More STORY MAKING!

Using Predictable Literature to Develop Communication

Robin E. Peura-Jones • Carolyn J. DeBoer

Thinking Publications
Eau Claire, Wisconsin

10   09   08   07   06   05   07   06   05   04   03

Library of Congress Cataloging-in-Publication Data

Peura, Robin E., date.
    More story making! : using predictable literature to develop communication / Robin E. Peura, Carolyn J. DeBoer.
       p. cm.
    Includes bibliographical references.
    ISBN 1-888222-55-7 (pbk.)
    1. Literature—Study and teaching (Early childhood) 2. Early childhood education—Activity programs. I. DeBoer, Carolyn J., date. II. Title.

LB1139.5.L58 P47 2000
372.6—dc21
                                                                    00-057762

Cover Design by Kris Madsen and Debbie Olson
Illustrations by Paul Modjeski

Printed in the United States of America

THINKING PUBLICATIONS®
A Division of McKinley Companies, Inc.

424 Galloway Street • Eau Claire, WI 54703
715.832.2488 • Fax 715.832.9082
Email: custserv@ThinkingPublications.com

COMMUNICATION SOLUTIONS THAT CHANGE LIVES®

All students can learn and succeed
but not on the same day in the same way.

William G. Spady

To my husband, Jim, for his love and support,
and to my children, Joshua and Hannah,
for the joy they bring as we watch them grow

REJ

To the memory of my loving parents, Margaret (Lancos)
and Michael Kochamba, for their constant encouragement,
praise, and support in all my educational endeavors

CJD

CONTENTS

Cross-Reference Charts

***More Story Making!* Pattern Books**

PREFACE

More Story Making! Using Predictable Literature to Develop Communication was written because we have developed a love and respect for children's literature, which stems from our work with children who have special needs. Through the years, we have continued to explore children's literature, as there is a wealth of books available for children to enjoy. In *More Story Making!* (as in *Story Making)*, we included a mix of contemporary and classic books that children enjoy. In our service delivery model, we have always recognized the need for meaningful teaching instead of a "drill and skill" method to motivate the students we serve. The predictable literature used in *More Story Making!* lends itself to the repetition that children need to hear as they practice and read their books. As children begin their journey with the printed word and are exposed to high-quality children's literature, we hope that they will develop a love for reading.

Through our combined efforts, *More Story Making!* should allow those who work with children to spend more time accomplishing child-centered goals and less time searching for information, activities, and materials. This resource will assist you in collaborative planning with classroom educators, parents, and caregivers. The objectives are cross-referenced to typical curricular themes and communication and thinking goals. Using *More Story Making!* in a classroom setting can help all children benefit from using literature to develop communication skills, concepts, and literacy.

We would like to thank the following people:

- The authors who wrote the predictable literature that proved to be the springboard for our ideas.

- Barb Pearson, for taking the time to help adapt information and for her many suggestions and encouragement.

- Our colleagues—Donna Hall, Sara Hanson, Teresa Caliguri, Marilyn Montgomery, and Dawn Falkowski—for all of their book suggestions that stem from their continued enthusiasm for children's literature.

- Kathy Niergarth, Title I Reading Coordinator, for her hours of explanations and for materials regarding literacy and reading at the elementary level.

- Paula Wassink, for her multiple intelligence workshops and the mnemonic "VAK."

- Maureen Abell and Regina Porter, for being part of a team that was truly collaborative and open to new ideas.

- Jeanne Smith and Rhonda Spyke, Beach School Secretaries, for their assistance in computer technology and for making sure all messages and mail were delivered.

- Our reviewers—Julie Early, Lisa Franks, Jamila Perry, and Linda Roth—for their time and insightful suggestions.

- Our editors—Nancy McKinley, Linda Schreiber, and Angie Sterling-Orth—and artist, Paul Modjeski, for their guidance and suggestions during our second journey into authorship.

- Our families—Jim, Joshua, Hannah, Garry, Carly, Amanda, and Sedona—for bearing with us while we were occupied with our full-time hobby: writing.

- Our parents, for providing us the foundation for learning in addition to their love and support, and our siblings—Luanne, David, and Michael—just because.

This joint adventure has been a journey as we have grown in many ways: acquiring knowledge, creating and experimenting with ideas, writing, editing, and learning our strengths and weaknesses (including the Internet). But, best of all, we have both found a dear friend.

ABOUT THE AUTHORS

Robin E. Peura-Jones is a speech-language pathologist with Hamilton County Educational Service Center in Ohio, where she primarily serves students in the Southwest Local School System. Robin works with children in preschool and elementary school with various disabilities in addition to case-managing the preschool children for the district. Robin has supervised graduate students from the University of Cincinnati and the University of New Mexico. She received her bachelor's and master's degrees in speech-language pathology from Bowling Green State University and holds her Certificate of Clinical Competence from the American Speech-Language-Hearing Association. Prior to returning to Ohio, Robin spent an extended time in Albuquerque, New Mexico, serving children in the Albuquerque Public Schools. Robin has conducted presentations locally, regionally, and nationally on topics including *Story Making,* "Classroom Materials and Techniques for Children with Autism/Spectrum Disorder," "Early Childhood Issues: Pervasive Developmental Disorders and Computers," "Literature-Based Activities for the SLP," "Curriculum-Based Strategies for Adolescents," and "A Transdisciplinary Team Approach to Early Childhood Intervention." She currently resides in Cincinnati, Ohio, with her husband, Jim, and their two children, Joshua and Hannah.

Carolyn J. DeBoer lives in western Michigan and works for the Fruitport Community Schools as a speech-language pathologist at the elementary and junior high levels. She has served as a mentor for graduate students, speech-language assistants, and beginning SLPs during their Clinical Fellowship Year. She worked as a school-based speech-language pathologist in New Jersey, Connecticut, and Ohio. She earned her bachelor's degrees in speech-language pathology and elementary education at Kean College of New Jersey and her master's degree in speech-language pathology from the University of Connecticut, Storrs. She is a member of the American Speech-Language-Hearing Association and holds her Certificate of Clinical

Competence. Carolyn has presented at the state, county, and local levels on topics including "Literature-Based Activities for the SLP," "Curriculum-Based Strategies for Adolescents," "Developing and Using Authentic Assessment," and "Accommodating SLI Students by Using Multiple Intelligence Activities in Learning." Recently, she received several local grants to develop intervention techniques using computer technology and phonological awareness skills. Carolyn lives with her husband, Garry, in Spring Lake, Michigan. Their two daughters, Carly and Amanda, are currently attending college in Alabama.

INTRODUCTION

Overview

More Story Making! Using Predictable Literature to Develop Communication provides activities to foster communication development in children from preschool through early elementary grades. *More Story Making!*—like its predecessor, *Story Making* (Peura and DeBoer, 1995)—uses predictable, repetitive sentences from children's favorite literature to generate child-authored stories. In these stories, sentences are repeated with slight wording changes. During the stories and accompanying activities, children receive multiple opportunities to hear and use targeted speech, language, and literacy models. Children can then take their pattern books home to read to others, which encourages further communication practice as well as language and literacy learning. *More Story Making!* improves children's communication and literacy skills and can enhance collaboration among professionals, parents, and other caregivers.

Story Making, the original book, provides 44 pattern stories. *More Story Making!* presents 47 all-new pattern stories and dozens of suggestions for additional activities. Like in *Story Making,* all the pattern stories and additional activities in *More Story Making!* are designed to target a wide array of goals for improving phonology, syntax, semantics, and thinking skills. In addition, literacy skills related to phonological awareness, reading, and writing are suggested. The stories are cross-referenced by specific curricular themes (e.g., transportation, time), so they can complement classroom activities. Reproducible materials—including pattern pages, 424 illustrations, forms for monitoring progress, parent resources and response forms, and a procedural outline—are provided for the educator's convenience.

More Story Making! Format

More Story Making! is structured so that stories, activities, patterns, illustrations, and forms can be located and used with ease. The following terms are referred to throughout this resource:

- *Model story*—a well-known children's book that contains a repetitive, predictable language pattern

- *Predictable pattern*—the repetitive sentence(s) that make up each model story and pattern book

- *Pattern book*—a variation of a model story that children create using the reproducible pattern pages and illustrations

- *Story profile*—the pages that explain a model story, its corresponding pattern book, the story goals, and the additional activities

More Story Making! taps into 30 model stories that contain repeating phonological, syntactic, and semantic patterns. Since many of these model stories are accompanied by two or more pattern stories, a total of 47 pattern books can be created. The pattern books and additional activities build on concepts and themes found in the model stories. Each of the pattern stories contains communication and cognitive goals, general themes, and suggestions for additional activities. A discussion of general procedures for using *More Story Making!* begins on page 35, and a reproducible, procedural outline is located in Appendix A.

The model story, pattern book(s), and additional activities described in each story profile can be used as an entire lesson or can be used to supplement existing lessons. The contents of the story profiles are further explained on page 62. When a story profile is used as the basis of a complete lesson:

1. The educator presents the model story.

2. Children create pattern books based on the model story and the predictable pattern.

3. One or more additional activities are conducted to extend learning and to provide repeated opportunities for use of targeted skills.

4. Several items are sent home, including pattern books, recommendations for use of children's literature, and items created during extension activities, to promote exposure to targeted language and literacy skills outside of the classroom.

Goals

The goals of *More Story Making!* cover a range of communication and literacy skills and include to:

- Facilitate development of phonology, syntax, and semantics through the use of children's literature, child-created pattern stories, and language-experience activities, which all combine to provide repeated exposure to and use of specific targets

- Provide children with early literacy experiences in reading (including phonological awareness), writing, listening, and speaking through the use of high-quality predictable children's literature

- Develop cognitive and metalinguistic skills through exposure to developmentally appropriate children's literature and problem-solving activities

- Link oral and written language tasks using a whole language approach

- Encourage collaborative teaching among educators, parents, and other caregivers to facilitate development of children's communication and literacy skills

- Provide parents and other caregivers with activities that link school learning to home situations

Target Audience

More Story Making! uses popular books that will appeal to many children. Pattern stories and additional activities associated with each model story are flexible enough to use with preschool children and those in primary grades (kindergarten through grade three). Preschool children will require more guidance when using *More Story Making!* while third graders might be more independent and creative with their work.

More Story Making! is useful for professionals working with children who have a wide range of needs, including children with language disorders, learning disabilities, phonological disorders, apraxia of speech, and autism, as well as children learning English as a second language. This resource is also excellent for general educators to use with students who are developing typically and are learning to read.

More Story Making! meets the needs of children in individual and group intervention settings and those involved in collaborative lessons in the classroom. The model stories, pattern books, and additional activities can easily be adapted to target classroom goals and individual children's needs.

Special Features

More Story Making! contains special features that contribute to its organized, easy-to-use, functional nature. Cross-reference charts are provided on pages 46–57 to aid in choosing stories for use. Each pattern book has been cross-referenced to goals for phonology, syntax, semantics, and thinking skills. In addition, the pattern books are cross-referenced to themes related to general curriculum areas (e.g., animals, food). The themes relate to children's classroom and real-life experiences, build on their knowledge of these experiences, and reinforce new concepts related to the themes.

The appendices in *More Story Making!* contain a variety of reproducible forms for monitoring progress, tracking activity use, and communicating with parents or other caregivers. Forms for monitoring progress in Appendix B allow educators to monitor the development of specific communication skills for individual children. The *Lesson Tracker* in Appendix C helps document and track lessons for individual children or small and large groups. These forms create a quick guide for reviewing student progress and planning future lessons. The *Parent Letter* in Appendix D, the *Parent Feedback* form in Appendix E, and the *Encouraging Literacy Skills at Home* letter in Appendix F are all provided to facilitate communication between school and home. The *Picture Index* in Appendix G makes it easy to locate each of the 424 illustrations so that they may be used interchangeably among stories and for additional activities.

BACKGROUND

Communication Development through Children's Literature

One of the greatest benefits of using literature as a foundation for targeting specific communication skills is the conversation that occurs before, while, and after reading a story. Books that target specific communication goals can be strategically selected. When books with repetitive patterns are chosen, children are exposed to the targeted communication goals multiple times. Therefore, use of stories with repetitive patterns provides a wonderful model for oral language in a functional and meaningful context. In addition, illustrations in storybooks help children increase understanding of concepts and vocabulary. Stories and pictures naturally elicit oral language as children comment, ask questions, and answer questions about what they hear and see. From these literacy activities, children can develop communication skills as well as reading skills, such as a sight vocabulary, sound-symbol knowledge, and spelling-pattern awareness.

Children acquire communication skills gradually. As children become more adept at using their communication skills and make the transition from oral to literate language, they begin to use concise syntax, explicit vocabulary, and cohesion based on explicit linguistic markers (Westby, 1991). They expand their basic sentence structures to include more ideas and details and use a variety of complex grammatical structures. Linguistic abilities can continue to emerge as children acquire a better understanding of a story through repeated exposure. The repetition of the story and conversations about it help children talk about familiar ideas and daily situations in increasingly complex ways (Norris and Damico, 1990).

Reading stories with children fosters vocabulary development, general language development, and interest and success in reading (Watson, Layton,

Pierce, and Abraham, 1994). Frequently rereading a story reproduces a verbal pattern of words that rapidly becomes predictable. Story retelling promotes narrative-discourse skills and story comprehension, which in turn support oral and written language development (Hoggan and Strong, 1994). Norris and Hoffman (1993) note, "Written language is useful in facilitating oral language because the print provides a visual, and therefore more contextualized, level of input that the child can use to organize oral language" (p. 223). As children's language structures become increasingly more complex, attention can be directed to higher-level communication skills, such as sequencing events, hypothesizing, making inferences, solving problems, identifying causes and effects, making associations, and comparing and contrasting. "Flexibility [in lesson organization] allows the child to develop the ability to reorganize and recombine concepts in thought and language. It allows the child to use the same language in a variety of different contexts" (Norris and Hoffman, 1993, p. 7).

More Story Making! provides children with opportunities to develop communication skills and to make the transition from oral to literate language. As model stories are read, children are repeatedly exposed to targeted linguistic and literacy skills. As children retell stories, create their own pattern books, and participate in related literacy activities, communication skills—including story comprehension and narrative discourse—are enhanced.

Literacy Acquisition
Early Literacy

In reference to communication, listening and speaking can be thought of as being on one side of the coin, with reading and writing on the other. The primary task for children entering school is to make the transition from oral to literate language. Many preschool children come to school having collected a wealth of literacy knowledge before they have actually learn to read (e.g., knowing how to hold a book, distinguishing between illustrations and text); this is known as *emergent literacy* (van Kleeck, 1990). Research shows that book, story, and print experiences that occur before school entry are crucial for later reading success (Allington and Cunningham, 1995).

Literacy skills begin developing at a very early age (1½ to 2 years), with skills continuing to build on one another as a child grows. In the initial stages, the behaviors or skills a child is learning are embedded in meaningful activities, with the adult taking responsibility for unfolding the activities.

> Adult input and direct scaffolding are necessary until the child has formed rather comprehensive mental responses of the event or activity. Studies, which looked at the impact of early literacy experiences on children's acquisition of various aspects of knowledge about print (van Kleeck, 1990) and metalinguistic skill development (van Kleeck, 1994), indicate the need for guidance and support by a literate person. As such, social transmission is critical to early stages of learning, whereas internal cognitive reorganization is emphasized later. (van Kleeck, 1994, p. 64)

Before formal schooling, children learn something about reading every time they are required to interact meaningfully with print. An adult focusing a child's attention on print through informal experiences, such as reading a sign or a postcard, gives the child knowledge of the meaningfulness of print. Theories on early acquisition of reading and writing processes suggest reading readiness has more to do with book, story, and print experiences that occur prior to formal schooling than with earlier reading-readiness and mental-age theories, which emphasized discrete skills (e.g., auditory discrimination, letter naming) (Allington and Cunningham, 1995). Westby (1991) suggests, "The objectives of the early stages [of literacy] are to expose students to a literate style of language and to structure opportunities that require specific use of language and facilitate the reporting of experiences" (p. 350).

Westby (1998) further states that by the middle elementary years, when children become dynamic and critical readers, they must be able to do the following:

1. Recognize individual words

2. Understand grammatical and semantic relations between words

3. Integrate ideas in the text, make inferences to aid integration, and fill in implicit information

Children without disabilities focus simultaneously on the form (i.e., structure) and the content (i.e., meaning) of their language by the age of 6 or 7.

Prior to that, they are able to attend to either the structure or the meaning separately, but not both at the same time (van Kleeck, 1995). The ability to simultaneously focus on both aspects of language facilitates the development of literacy skills.

Factors Affecting Literacy Development

Early interactions with print through reading and writing enhance the learning environment for all children, especially children with language disorders (Watson et al., 1994). The opportunity to experiment with print and to relate print forms with speech acts is crucial to building literacy skills such as reading, writing, listening, and speaking. Children require repetitive practice with literacy activities along with adult scaffolding to develop these skills (McFadden, 1998). In addition, children need to feel comfortable and safe when making errors or experimenting with language form and meaning. Johnson and Louis (1990) note that "Children need relevant, interesting, and achievable experiences with literacy in warm, tolerant, supportive, and forgiving environments" (p. 7). When too many demands are placed on children, they do not participate, causing them to have limited practice with literature and linguistic structures.

Language disorders are thought to be an underlying factor in reading and most other literacy-learning difficulties (Kamhi and Catts, 1991; Stanovich, Cunningham, and Freeman, 1984; Watson et al., 1994). In determining the causal factors of failure to learn to read, Stanovich et al. (1984) found that in early reading acquisition, multiple factors, not just intelligence, were responsible for predicting reading success in grades one, three, and five. *Phonological awareness* (i.e., the ability to break speech up into smaller units of words, syllables, and sounds), decoding speed, and listening comprehension (including real-world knowledge, inferential skills, memory strategies, and vocabulary) were major determinants in successful reading comprehension after general intelligence was considered (Stanovich et al., 1994). In particular, young children with speech-language disorders have been described as being at high risk for difficulties in learning to read and write (Wallach and Butler, 1994).

More Story Making! provides low-pressure activities in which children are allowed to experiment and learn through their play with language. A familiar storybook context and adult scaffolding allow children to participate in the language activities and gradually gain competence over the tasks and the language skills involved.

Literacy Development through Children's Literature

The use of children's literature for class reading and writing instruction helps create interest in literacy (Creaghead, 1992). Children who are read to during their preschool years find it to be a pleasurable activity and an avenue for learning new information. Sharing nursery rhymes, playground rhythms, selected poems, and pattern stories with repetition, refrains, and cumulative chants is fun for children. These types of shared experiences form a bridge for the transition from an emerging reader to a developing reader.

Quality literacy activities should be relevant to children's experiences and should be directed at developing all modes of communication. Literacy skills are important as a means of expression and enhanced communication, an aid for learning and memory, and a vehicle for the enjoyment of language (Owens and Robinson, 1997). Shared reading, with its interactive nature of talk and activity, enhances literacy development (Morrow and O'Connor, 1995). Johnson and Louis (1990) note that "Materials for shared reading should be meaningful, memorable, good quality literature which is highly structured, short, energetic, robust, and rhythmically repetitive" (p. 17). By having books read to them, children learn to deal with meaningful aspects of their lives. If literacy events are meaningful, normal, regular, and reasonably frequent, literacy behavior will develop (Johnson and Louis).

Fostering Reading Skills

It takes much more than simply reading books to children to develop their reading skills. Adults must share books with children while conversing about the content and the form of the story. Reading aloud should be an interactive, reciprocal activity with child participation, shared reading, and discussion (Owens and Robinson, 1997). To ensure success for beginning readers, Luedeker (1996) uses the following "early literacy elements": reading stories aloud, independent reading, shared reading, guided reading, interactive and shared writing, and independent writing. In addition, the invaluable experiences of reading aloud, conducting interactive language activities, and using predictable books should be supplemented with activities in phonemic awareness, which draws children's attention to a critical aspect of their language development and early reading success (Yopp, 1992).

More Story Making! activities that center around shared reading provide opportunities for children to experiment with and develop communication and reading skills. The use of pattern books in shared reading activities helps each child make the transition from an emerging reader to a developing reader. Through the repeated use of the model stories and the pattern stories, children are given a foundation for developing Luedeker's (1996) early literacy elements.

Fostering Writing Skills

Writing skills also have a place in early literacy development, long before formal reading instruction begins. Parents who foster a literate home environment by participating in shared reading during the preschool years allow reading and writing to grow along with listening and speaking skills, rather than after such oral language skills are developed (Allington and Cunningham, 1995). Children's early writing attempts are often encouraged by the books they encounter. Books with repetitive, predictable patterns provide written models that are easy for children to reproduce.

Sulzby (1989) identifies six major categories that exemplify the writing productions of kindergartners: (1) writing via drawing, (2) writing via scribbling, (3) letterlike forms, (4) well-learned units, (5) invented spelling, and (6) conventional spelling. All six categories represent information that children are communicating through what they write.

More Story Making! provides activities that encourage creativity and imagination through written language as children author and illustrate their own books. Children can attempt to write their responses in the blanks and draw corresponding illustrations (i.e., the pattern books can be customized to account for a wide variety of writing levels and skills).

Predictable Stories

Cumulative, repetitive, predictable stories are effective tools for beginning the transition from oral to literate language (Westby, 1991). In predictable stories, a phrase or sentence is repeated while one or more of the words are changed. Table 1 lists several reasons for using predictable stories. The familiar content, repetitive structure, and cyclical sequencing of events make these types of stories appealing to children (Goodman, 1986).

Repetitive, developmentally appropriate patterns help children understand and produce language and predict and infer in an authentic context (Montgomery, 1993). The repetition of the phrase and sentence patterns in predictable literature also gives children opportunities to listen to, anticipate, and produce the patterns. These features of repetitive literature give children a context that reduces their cognitive load and allows them to focus their attention on features that might not be attended to when reading unfamiliar stories (McFadden, 1998). These features also allow children to focus on complex semantic-syntactic relationships by increasing their understanding of the semantic relationships in the story (Bradshaw, Hoffman, and Norris, 1998).

Table 1
Predictable Stories—Why Use Them?
They are high-interest, so they:
• Become the stories children request time and again • Appeal to children's natural enjoyment of rhyme and rhythm
They are repetitive, so they:
• Create opportunities for children to listen to, anticipate, predict, and produce the contained language patterns • Become a model for reading and writing new stories • Allow children to make comments about the story, rather than just ask and answer questions • Reduce the cognitive demands of attending to both the content and the form of the story • Become easy for students to read and are easily memorized • Facilitate the transition from oral to literate language use

Sources: Bradshaw et al. (1998); Martinez and Roser (1985); Montgomery (1993); Routman (1991); Westby (1991).

The predictable patterns in *More Story Making!* develop specific communication skills and early literacy skills through the use of the model stories and child-created pattern books. Once a particular pattern becomes familiar, children can retell and write a parallel version of the model story—which is the basis of *More Story Making!*

Repeated Readings

Martinez and Roser (1985) found that children begin to attend to different aspects of a story after repeated readings by a teacher or parent. In their study, the quality and range of the children's responses changed with increasing familiarity with a story. These researchers found that repeated readings lead children to talk more about a story; make comments, rather than just ask or answer questions; focus responses on events, details, setting, and theme; and increase processing (i.e., make associations between characters and gain greater insight into the story). Repeated readings therefore allow children to produce more divergent responses.

Many children who rarely or never respond to questions will often supply answers when a *cloze technique* is used, especially after a predictable story is read several times. A cloze technique provides a child with a portion of an utterance that he or she might then be able to complete. For example, if the goal is for the child to respond with single words, the adult might say, "Hannah, Hannah, what do you hear? I hear a—" Then the adult waits to see if the child provides an appropriate response (e.g., *train).* Adults can also use a cloze technique to facilitate children's responses to a higher level of language complexity. For example, if a child primarily uses three-word utterances, the adult might say, "The very hungry bear ate—" and the child might respond, "Fish, but still hungry." After repeated readings of well-known model stories, *More Story Making!* leads to the creation of new stories and the generation of more complex responses.

Metalinguistic Skills

As children talk about what they have read, they expand their *metalinguistic skills*—skills used to reflect on and talk about language (Haynes and Shulman, 1994). Metalinguistic skills emerge when a child begins to distinguish print from nonprint (around 1½ to 2 years of age) and continue to develop into adulthood (Wallach and Miller, 1988). Table 2 outlines a general progression of metalinguistic development from 1½ to 10 years of age.

Table 2

Metalinguistic Development in Children

Stage One (Ages 1½ to 2)

- Distinguishes print from nonprint
- Knows how to interact with books: (i.e., right side up, page turning from right to left [sic])
- Recognizes some printed symbols, e.g., TV characters' names, brand names, signs

Stage Two (Ages 2 to 6)

- Ascertains word boundaries in spoken sentences
- Ascertains word boundaries in printed sequences
- Engages in word substitution play
- Plays with the sounds of language
- Begins to talk about language parts or [sic] about talking (speech acts)
- Corrects own speech/language to help the listener understand the message (spontaneously or in response to listener request)
- Self-monitors own speech and makes changes to more closely approximate the adult model; phonological first, lexical and semantic speech style last
- Believes that a word is an integral part of the object to which it refers (i.e., word realism)
- Able to separate words into syllables
- Inability to consider that one word could have two different meanings

Stage Three (Ages 6 to 10)

- Begins to take listener perspective and use language form to match
- Understands verbal humor involving linguistic ambiguity, e.g., riddles
- Able to resolve ambiguity: lexical first, as in homophones; deep structures next, as in ambiguous phrases ("Will you join me in a bowl of soup?"); phonological or morphemic next (Q: "What do you have if you put three ducks in a box?" A: "A box of quackers")
- Able to understand that words can have two meanings, one literal and the other non-conventional or idiomatic (e.g., adjectives used to describe personality characteristics such as *hard, sweet, bitter)*
- Able to resequence language elements, as in pig Latin
- Able to segment syllables into phonemes
- Finds it difficult to appreciate figurative forms other than idioms

From *Language Intervention and Academic Success* (p. 33), by G. Wallach and L. Miller, 1988, Newton, MA: Butterworth Heinemann. © 1988 by Butterworth Heinemann. Reprinted with permission.

Metalinguistic skills can be enhanced while reading to children. Metalinguistic skills are targeted when adults draw children's attention to and comment on specific features, such as how a book is being held, the names of letters that correspond with those in a child's name, and the presence of humor and word play in a story. These activities not only assist children in acquiring language and literacy knowledge, but also develop a child's metalinguistic skills.

Children who have language and learning difficulties are often limited to using language for social discourse functions and lack the metalinguistic orientation to support the development of literate language forms needed for academic reading and writing tasks (van Kleeck, 1994). This stresses the importance of exposing children to metalinguistic activities that lead to oral language and literacy necessary for school success.

In *More Story Making!* stories are cross-referenced based on thinking (i.e., metalinguistic) skills. Thinking sills can be highlighted when reading a model story, creating pattern books, and conducting one or more of the recommended additional activities.

Phonological Awareness

Development

Much has been written about phonological awareness—a form of metalinguistic skill—in relation to students with reading disorders and language disorders. Goswami and Bryant (1990) define *phonological awareness* as knowing how words and syllables can be broken down into their smaller units. Goldsworthy (1996) states, "The terms *linguistic awareness, phonological awareness, phoneme awareness, phoneme segmentation,* or *phonemic analysis* are used interchangeably in the literature. They refer to the metalinguistic ability that allows a language user to perceive spoken words as consisting of a series of individual speech sounds" (p. 67).

Phonological awareness skills are significantly related to reading abilities in children both with and without language disorders (Swank and Catts, 1994). Children's letter-sound knowledge and phonemic awareness skills are the strongest predictors of their future reading success (Rivers, Lombardino, and Thompson, 1996). For many children, these skills develop without specific instruction (Stackhouse, 1997). Rhyming and syllable segmentation are the first phonological awareness skills to emerge (Liberman, Shankweiler, Fischer, and Carter, 1974), and sound manipulation and cluster segmentation are the last skills to emerge (Stackhouse). Phonological awareness skills identified as strongly related to reading development include sound deletion, sound and word categorizing, sound segmentation, sound blending, and nursery rhyme knowledge (Gilbertson and Bramlett, 1998). Table 3 (on page 16) describes the general developmental progression of phonological awareness skills.

Intervention

Studies of prereaders indicate that the best way to stimulate phonological awareness skills is through familiar oral language games, nursery rhymes, and frequent book sharing (Friel-Patti, 1998). Van Kleeck, Gillam, and McFadden (1998) indicate:

> Rhyming (a) is an activity that sensitizes children to the sound structure of words, (b) is a naturally occurring activity among many preschoolers, (c) is often quite difficult for children with language and speech impairments, (d) is an ability that predicts later reading and spelling ability, (e) seems to contribute to later reading and spelling independent of its relationship to phoneme awareness, and (f) has been effectively used in previous studies that trained phonological awareness skills in children. (p. 67)

Specific phonological awareness goals need to be addressed during intervention with children (both preschool and school-age) who have language disorders and who are at risk for reading difficulties. In the Phonological Awareness Group Education (PAGE) intervention program (Gilbertson and Thompson, 1997), students worked on goals in phonological awareness, syntax, semantics, and pragmatics using a format that included predictable books that could be read aloud by the children. The PAGE project found that many of the students showed improvement in phonological awareness skills as well as word recognition and reading comprehension abilities.

Gillon (2000) studied students who had expressive language disorders, phonological difficulties, and early reading delays, during their participation in an integrated phonological awareness program. Her findings suggest that

Table 3

Phonological Awareness Development

By age 3, children typically can:

- Recite familiar rhymes (e.g., *Pat-a-Cake)*
- Recognize alliteration (e.g., "*P*op and *p*ig are the same")

By age 4, children typically can:

- Spontaneously use rhyming-word combinations (e.g., "Daddy, listen: *cat, hat, sat, bat.* They're the same!")
- Produce multisyllabic words while separating the syllables (e.g., "I can say the word *elephant* like this: *el • e • phant.* That's funny!")

By age 5, children typically can:

- Count the number of syllables in words (e.g., "*Cucumber* is a long word. *Cu • cum • ber.* It has three parts")

By age 6, children typically can:

- Tell a word that rhymes with a given word (e.g., "*Tape* rhymes with *cape")*
- Blend 2 or 3 sounds to form words (e.g., "*B • e • d* says *bed")*
- Count the number of sounds in words (e.g., "*D • o • g.* That has three sounds")
- Segment the initial sound from words to match other words (e.g., recognizing that *man, mop,* and *milk* all start with the same sound)
- Segment the initial sound from words to create new words (e.g., knowing that if /k/ is removed from the word *cup,* the new word is *up)*

By age 7, children typically can:

- Blend more than 3 sounds to form words (e.g., "*D • a • dd • y* says *daddy")*
- Segment 3 or 4 sounds in words (e.g., "*Pillow.* That has four sounds: *p • i • ll • ow")*
- Spell simple words phonetically (e.g., *kat* for *cat)*
- Remove phonemes from words to make new words (e.g., "*Date* without /t/ is *day")*

Sources: Goldsworthy, 1998; Hall and Moats, 1999; Snow, Scarborough, and Burns, 1999; Stackhouse, 1997.

students who received phonological awareness intervention made significantly more gains in their phonological and articulation skills and reading abilities than did students who participated in language intervention services without a phonological awareness component. Intervention programs that target phonological awareness, word meaning, and word structure should be integrated into curricular activities that include reading and spelling at a level appropriate for each child's level of literacy (Lombardino, Riccio, Hynd, and Pinheiro, 1997).

More Story Making! can be used to facilitate and reinforce a wide range of phonological awareness skills. Many of the model books and corresponding pattern books chosen to be included in this resource contain rhythmic and rhyming patterns that can help students recognize the sound similarities in words. *More Story Making!* incorporates a holistic approach that uses predictable, repetitive structures with contextual vocabulary to address phonological awareness. Although specific phonological awareness skills are not stated in each story profile, many of the story profiles include an additional activity designed to target phonological awareness. Table 4 (on pages 18–19) demonstrates how the activities in *More Story Making!* can be adapted to highlight an array of phonological awareness skills.

Whole Language Philosophy

The philosophy of whole language looks at communication as a whole rather than as separate components. Listening, speaking, reading, and writing are viewed as interdependent. Both oral and written language are viewed as functions of communication, and comprehension and production of oral and written language are viewed as one process. Whole language philosophy integrates all elements of communication into a curriculum. Classrooms implementing whole language philosophy are child-centered, literature-based, talk-focused, active, parent-involved, fun, and varied (Creaghead, 1992). "Whole language specialists contend that the written and oral modes of language have transactional effects on one another, such that oral language can be enhanced through reading and writing and vice versa" (Watson et al., 1994, p. 137).

Table 4	
Phonological Awareness Activities	

Beginning Skills

1. ***Count the words*** in a predictable pattern.
   - Have students draw a line, slide a chip across a table, clap, or hold up a finger for each word they hear.

     Example: *"Let's count the words in the first sentence. Hold up one finger each time you hear a word. Listen, Chicka Chicka Boom Boom!* [Hold up one finger as each new word is said.] *Look, we have four fingers up, there are four words in that sentence."*

   - Assist students with placing a dot below each word and then point to each word as the pattern is read.

     Example: *The very hungry bear ate 1 fish, but he was still hungry.*
     • • • • • • • • • • • • •

2. ***Generate rhyming words*** for selected words.
   - Write a word where everyone can see it (also include the predictable pattern when appropriate) and list the rhyming words that children generate below the target word, so that the rimes line up and the rhyming pattern is visible.

     Example: *Bubbles, bubbles all around. Some just landed on my* **cat**.
     > ***hat***
     > ***mat***
     > ***flat***
     > ***splat***

   - Provide children with a word and tell them to think of a word that rhymes with the given word.

     Example: *"Use a word that rhymes with* big *to finish the sentence on the first page of your book."*

Intermediate Skills

1. ***Count the syllables*** in a predictable pattern or word.
   - Have students draw a line, slide a chip across a table, clap, or hold up a finger for each syllable they hear.

     Example: *"Salamander is a long word. Let's clap one time for each part in the word. Listen:* Sal • a • man • der. *That's four parts!"*

   - Assist students with placing a dot below each syllable and then point to each syllable as the pattern is read.

     Example: *Zicka zicka zoom zoom!*
     • • • • • •

Table 4—*Continued*

2. ***Blend word parts*** (i.e., syllables).
   - Pronounce words in separated form and ask students to blend the word parts and tell the word.
     Example: *"What word do these parts make:* el • e • phant?*"*

Advanced Skills

1. ***Segment words into parts*** (i.e., syllables or sounds).
   - Count the phonemes in single words. Have children draw a line, slide a chip across a table, clap, or hold up a finger for each sound they hear in a word.
     Example: *"Let's count the sounds in the word* cat. *Make one line on your paper each time you hear a sound. Listen:* C • a • t. *Look, do you have three marks on your paper? Terrific!"*
   - Pronounce words and ask students to segment the words into parts.
     Examples: *"Break this word into parts:* porcupine.*"* (por • cu • pine)
     "Break this word apart into its sounds: pig.*"* (p • i • g)

2. ***Match initial, medial, or final sounds*** in words.
   - Gradually reveal each sound in a word, having students blend the sounds to figure out the word. Then have students use the blended word in a pattern phrase.
     Example: *"Blend the sounds I say to figure out the word you should use to complete the last sentence on your page. 'Candy for sale. Fifty cents a candy. I want a r • e • d candy.' Blend r • e • d to figure out what kind of candy I want."*
   - Tell children to use a particular sound to complete a pattern phrase.
     Example: *"Today when we make our pattern books, we will only use words that begin with the /t/ sound."*

3. ***Manipulate sounds*** in words.
   - Have children say a target word from the story. Then tell them a sound to delete. Have them say the new word.
     Example: *"Bear without /b/ is air?"*

Some children are not successful in school, because they are unable to meet all the language demands of the curriculum (i.e., the content of information in the classroom). Johnson and Louis (1990) explain:

Whole language programs offer texts which, although they may be conceptually simple, are at least as linguistically complex as the oral language of the children. They encourage children to make language of the text their own through a series of meaningful, open-ended activities. The richness of the language and the open-ended nature of the activities permit individuals to learn those aspects of written language they are "ready" to learn. (p. 9)

More Story Making! applies whole language philosophy to language learning. Participation is maximized as children are encouraged to read along, predict events, and supply a range of appropriate answers. Children attend to language form and content, including the sounds of the predictable pattern, as they listen to and then use this language in an oral and written form while participating in an array of literacy and language activities.

Collaboration

As schools implement a variety of inclusion models, educators must collaborate more and more. Collaboration is a fundamental way of working in a true partnership to share methods, understand student learning styles, and develop strategies for student success. As educators work together to enhance students' functioning in natural learning environments, new ideas develop, and the benefits to children are obvious. The child with a language-learning disorder is served best by collaboration among professionals and between professionals and parents (Marvin and Privratsky, 1999; Marvin and Wright, 1997; Westby, 1991). Stainback and Stainback (1992) say that "Without this collaboration, inclusive education cannot be successful since inclusion is predicated on professionals working together for the purpose of enhancing all the students in the school" (p. 85). Collaboration helps meet the changing needs of all children while following the child-centered objectives of the curriculum.

More Story Making! meets the needs of educators who are using collaborative models of teaching. When using this resource in a classroom setting, it can be adapted to address each child's needs. During a single lesson, children in the same group can focus on a variety of skills. Speech intelligibility, language structures (i.e., syntax), vocabulary development, thinking skills, phonological awareness skills, beginning reading skills, and writing skills can be infused into each lesson designed with *More Story Making!* Thus, the same activity can be used to accomplish a variety of goals, depending on each child's needs. *More Story Making!* facilitates collaboration among educational professionals, especially between the classroom teacher and the speech-language pathologist, and between educators and parents.

Home Involvement

Language learning and literacy development are lifelong processes begun at home and continued in all of a child's interactive environments (Koppenhaver, Coleman, Kalman, and Yoder, 1991). Parents are considered the most familiar and influential communication partners for children learning to talk (Marvin and Privratsky, 1999). In addition, parents play a vital role at the preschool stage by sharing literacy events with their children (Goodman, 1986). During the routines of daily living—such as shopping, playing, pretending, cleaning, and cooking—language and literacy development are encouraged.

Children come to school with different degrees of exposure to language models and literature. The difference between "home language" and "school language" will frequently result in gaps between ability and performance in class (Simon, 1991). Due to extraordinary circumstances and/or a lack of parental awareness, some preschool children have less opportunity at home and at school to interact with literacy-related materials (Koppenhaver et al., 1991; Marvin and Mirenda, 1992; Marvin and Wright, 1997; Norris and Damico, 1990). Marvin (1994) suggests that the presence of any disability can significantly influence parental expectations and the opportunities provided to children to be socialized toward literacy at home. The presence of multiple disabilities puts children at greatest risk for limited exposure to literacy activities. Differences in cultural backgrounds can also place a child in an at-risk situation in adapting to school language and school scripts (i.e., school routines) (Simon, 1991). The resulting limited literacy experience of these children has a strong relationship to later difficulties in reading and writing skills (Catts, 1993).

Children begin to make the transition from oral to literate language in the preschool years. Early childhood programs promote the integration of learning through the use of themes at school by encouraging children to bring meaningful contributions from home experiences related to school themes (Wetherby, 1992). This integration allows children to develop narrative ability and to talk about things familiar to them (e.g., home, play, nature), thereby helping children make the oral to literate language transition. In the same manner, materials young children carry home from preschool appear to have a significant, positive effect on their talk with parents after school (Marvin and Privratsky, 1999).

Parents who frequently interact with and read to their children help develop the language and literacy skills that will contribute to social and academic success. Parents can provide stimulating and supportive contexts for developing language and literacy by praising vocalizations, using eye gazes, and gesturing during reading and writing events; rephrasing questions and commenting about stories and pictures for more successful interactions; and recognizing that daily routines have literacy opportunities (Marvin and Wright, 1997). Parents can also provide what is known as *scaffolding dialogue,* that is, asking children questions and providing answers when children cannot answer (Westby, 1991). The interaction time a parent and child spend together reading a book can be an enormously positive experience that complements learning at school.

Use of *decontextualized speech*—talking about activities that occurred in a different situation or context (e.g., when a parent says to a child, "Can you show me how to make a paper-bag puppet like the one you made in school today?")—also allows for subsequent learning. Decontextualized speech is an essential skill that children begin to acquire at approximately 4 years of age, as they gain the ability to discuss events from the past or in the future. Many children with language disorders have difficulty using decontextualized speech (Wallach and Miller, 1988). Repeating the same information, story, or procedure to different listeners can help these children bridge the transition from home to school and strengthen the home-to-school link (Norris and Hoffman, 1993). Knowledge of a child's recent experiences will help a parent engage the child in a conversation that is interesting to the child, thus leading to extended conversation that furthers development of advanced communication skills (Marvin and Privratsky, 1999).

More Story Making! provides several opportunities to involve parents and other caregivers in children's language and literacy development. The pattern books children create, and any other items they make or verbally practice during follow-up activities, can be discussed at home so that generalization of communication goals, literacy skills, and thematic targets occurs in a familiar environment. The pattern book provides a communication environment for the child; that is, it provides a reason for communicating. Bringing home the personalized pattern books facilitates children's talking about their school experiences. Each *More Story Making!* pattern book can serve as a visual reminder of experiences children have had during the school day and can facilitate use of decontextualized speech at home.

More Story Making! also provides the home-to-school link to literacy. As children repeatedly read their pattern books, literacy skills emerge. Appendix F provides other helpful tips for infusing literacy experiences throughout a child's day. It can be reproduced and shared with parents and other caregivers.

Assessment of Communication Skills
Authentic Assessment

Educational specialists use an array of techniques when evaluating children, some of which are standardized and some of which are not. Evaluations that overemphasize standardized scores and overlook daily work samples, observations of the child in the classroom, and parental feedback are not always relevant. Larson and McKinley (1995) remind professionals, "A standardized test that is supposedly objective cannot be considered worthwhile and valid if it is not assessing relevant behaviors in relevant situations" (p. 118). Therefore, diagnostic testing should include authentic procedures that focus on performance in the context of what students do, say, and make, as well as their effectiveness and efficiency in these tasks (Secord, 1999). Assessment should relate to a student's present level of performance, make improvements in instruction, and lead to outcome statements that are directly tied to real-life measures (Secord, 1999).

Speech-language pathologists determine if a child is an effective communicator across a wide variety of settings and situations. "Variables such as the interaction partner, conversational and discourse parameters, materials, setting, task, and information processing have become important aspects of a clinical evaluation" (Schraeder, Quinn, Stockman, and Miller, 1999, p. 196).

Authentic assessment occurs "when students are expected to perform, produce, or otherwise demonstrate skills that represent realistic learning demands...the contexts of the assessments are real-life settings in and out of the classroom without contrived and standardized conditions" (Udvari and Thousand as cited in Schraeder et al., 1999, p. 196).

Authentic assessment practices hold enormous potential for changing what is taught, how it is taught, and how children come to be readers and writers. Information from authentic assessment in conjunction with standardized assessment information, can be used to develop intervention plans and to monitor progress. Observations, samples of a child's work, and feedback from those who observe the child on a daily basis at school and at home can be used to write goals and instructional objectives.

Dynamic Assessment

Assessment should not only be authentic, but also dynamic, or what the "individual can learn when the proper scaffolding and mediation are provided" (Nelson, 1994, p. 113). In dynamic assessment, assessment and intervention happen concurrently and educators adapt to meet the needs of children. "Static procedures focus on products of assessment, revealing only those abilities that are completely developed [while dynamic assessment] refers to a number of approaches characterized by guided learning for the purpose of determining a learner's potential for change" (Brown and Campione as cited in Goldsworthy, 1996, p. 93).

Assessment of children's skills should be considered a daily activity and should be incorporated into all lessons. Fountas and Pinnell (1996) suggest that assessment:

- Be conducted as a part of daily teaching

- Include systematic observations that constantly update a child's profile

- Provide reliable and valid information

- Be multidimensional

- Contribute ways to improve instruction and curriculum

- Identify specific strategies to use with students who do not achieve despite excellent classroom instruction

- Involve children and parents in the process

These suggestions ensure assessment is dynamic, accurate, and useful.

Assessment with *More Story Making!*

More Story Making! can facilitate authentic, dynamic assessment. During *More Story Making!* activities, the context in which children use language to talk, read, and write is authentic in nature. The stories and activities provide meaningful contexts, pragmatic interactions, and relevant tasks in which to observe and evaluate desired communication and literacy skills. Furthermore, as stories are read to students, as students create and read their own books, and as students participate in additional activities, targeted behaviors can be observed and then recorded using the forms in Appendix B.

Parent's observations of their children's use of skills at home can be communicated through the *Parent Feedback* form (see Appendix E). Feedback from parents and other caregivers contributes to the authenticity of evaluative judgments regarding children's strengths and weaknesses.

Using *More Story Making!*

Choosing a Pattern Book

Pattern books should be selected for use with children after assessment has been completed, needs have been determined, and specific goals have been developed. Measurable objectives should also be developed for each student based on the goals.

A variety of goals can be targeted simultaneously with *More Story Making!* while children listen to model stories, create and read pattern books, and participate in additional activities. Suggested goals are provided on pages 41–43 for these goal areas: phonology, syntax, semantics, thinking skills, themes, and literacy. The goals provided are those typically addressed with children in preschool through early elementary grades. However, other goal areas related to communication (e.g., interaction skills, use of augmentative communication, listening skills) can also be addressed using this resource. Draw from the wealth of materials and ideas provided in *More Story Making!* to target goals not specifically stated.

Once goals are determined, refer to the easy-to-use cross-reference charts on pages 46–57 to locate pattern books that focus on specific goals. Table 5, beginning on page 28, provides information about the model stories and their corresponding pattern books. Publisher information is provided for each model story. A description of each goal area follows.

Targeting Communication Goals

Phonology Goals

More Story Making! supports a phonological process approach and a traditional articulation approach to remediation of phonological errors. Analysis of a child's phonological system is necessary before determining the approach to use and the goals for intervention.

Table 5

More Story Making!
Literature List

Model Story	*More Story Making!* Pattern Book(s)
Animals Should Definitely Not Act Like People (1989) by Judi Barrett New York: Aladdin	*Animals Should Definitely Not*
None	*Bubbles!*
But Not Like Mine (1988) by Margery Facklam New York: Harcourt Brace	*But Not Like Mine*
Caps for Sale (1999) by Esphyr Slobodkina New York: HarperCollins	*For Sale*
Chicka Chicka Boom Boom (1989) by Bill Martin, Jr., and John Archambault New York: Simon and Schuster	*Zicka Zicka Zoom Zoom!*
Cookie's Week (1997) by Cindy Ward New York: Putnam	*Kid's Day*
A Dark, Dark Tale (1992) by Ruth Brown New York: E.P. Dutton	*A Dark, Dark Cave* *A Hot, Hot Desert*
Each Peach Pear Plum (1999) by Janet and Allan Ahlberg New York: Penguin	*Each Pickle Pumpkin Pie*

Table 5—*Continued*

Model Story	*More Story Making!* Pattern Book(s)
Five Little Monkeys Sitting in a Tree (1999) by Eileen Christelow New York: Houghton Mifflin	*Five Little Monkeys*
Froggy Gets Dressed (1997) by Jonathon London New York: Viking	*Stanley Gets Ready for School!*
From Head to Toe (1999) by Eric Carle New York: HarperTrophy	*From Here to There*
Go Away, Big Green Monster! (1993) by Ed Emberly Boston: Little, Brown	*Come and Play, Friend!* *Come and Play, Creature!* *Come and Play, Animal Friend!*
Green Eggs and Ham (1960) by Dr. Seuss New York: Random House	*Blue Spaghetti and Meatballs*
Hi, Pizza Man! (1998) by Virginia Walter New York: Orchard Books	*Hi, Pizza Boy! (Animals)* *Hi, Pizza Boy! (Seasonal Characters)*
I Love You, Mouse (1990) by John Graham New York: Harcourt Brace	*I Like You, Animals* *I Like You, Colors*
Itchy, Itchy Chicken Pox (1992) by Grace MacCarone New York: Scholastic	*Itchy, Itchy Mosquito Bites!*
I've Been Working on the Railroad (1996) by Nadine Bernard Westcott New York: Hyperion	*I've Been Working on My House* *I've Been Working at My School*

Continued on next page

Table 5—*Continued*

Model Story	*More Story Making!* Pattern Book(s)
Jesse Bear, What Will You Wear? (1996) by Nancy White Carlstrom New York: Little Simon	*Carly Bear, What Will You Wear?*
The Judge (1988) by Harve Zemach New York: Farrar, Straus and Giroux	*My Pet Dog* *My Pet Cat*
The Little Engine That Could (1990) by Wally Piper New York: Price Stern Sloan	*I Think I Can, I Think I Can! (Sports)* *I Think I Can, I Think I Can! (Chores)*
The Mitten (1989) adapted and illustrated by Jan Brett New York: Putnam	*The Boat* *The Sled*
The Napping House (1984) by Audrey Wood New York: Harcourt Brace	*A Busy Farm*
No, David! (1998) by David Shannon New York: Scholastic	*It's Not Safe!*
Oh, A-Hunting We Will Go (1991) by John Langstaff New York: Aladdin	*To the Zoo We'll Go* *A-Riding We Will Go* *A-Shopping We Will Go*
One Bright Monday Morning (1962) by Arline and Joseph Baum New York: Random House	*One Bright Fall Morning*

Table 5—*Continued*

Model Story	*More Story Making!* Pattern Book(s)
Polar Bear, Polar Bear, What Do You Hear? (1997) by Bill Martin, Jr. New York: Holt	*Hannah, Hannah, What Do You Hear?* *Amanda, Amanda, What Do You Taste?*
Quick as a Cricket (1990) by Audrey Wood Swindon, UK: Child's Play	*I Am Me! (People)* *I Am Me! (Transportation)* *I Am Me! (Dogs)*
Silly Sally (1999) by Audrey Wood New York: Red Wagon Books	*Jolly Joshua* *Showy Shelly*
Time to Sleep (1997) by Denise Fleming New York: Holt	*Time for Spring!*
The Very Hungry Caterpillar (1994) by Eric Carle New York: Philomel Books	*The Very Hungry Bear*
Who Walks on This Halloween Night? (1998) by Harriet Ziefart New York: Little Simon	*Who Walks in the Zoo at Night?* *Who Moves in the Forest at Night?*

Phonological Processes Approach—The phonological process goals referenced in *More Story Making!* are based on Bankson and Bernthal's (1990) phonological process approach to remediation. Bankson and Bernthal identify 10 phonological processes as the most frequently used by young children: assimilation, fronting, final consonant deletion (FCD), weak syllable deletion (WSD), stopping, gliding, cluster simplification (CS), depalatalization, deaffrication, and vocalization. Bankson and Bernthal define these phonological processes as follows:

- Assimilation—replacement of one sound that is the same or similar to a second sound occurring elsewhere in the word *(tat* for *cat)*

- Fronting—replacement of a velar sound with one produced further forward in the mouth *(teep* for *keep)*

- Final consonant deletion—deletion of a final consonant singleton sound in a word *(too* for *tooth)*

- Weak syllable deletion—deletion of an unstressed (weak) syllable in a word *(bafla* for *butterfly, kanroo* for *kangaroo)*

- Stopping—replacement of a stop sound for a fricative, an affricate, or occasionally for a liquid sound *(but* for *bus)*

- Gliding—replacement of a glide for a prevocalic liquid sound *(wed* for *red)*

- Cluster simplification—reduction of a consonant cluster by deletion of one of the consonant sounds *(tick* for *stick);* replacement of a cluster with a single, different consonant sound *(wed* for *bread);* replacement of a consonant sound in a cluster with a different consonant sound *(vesht* for *vest);* or omission of a consonant cluster altogether *(een* for *green)*

- Depalatalization—replacement of a palatal sound with one produced further forward in the mouth *(seep* for *sheep)*

- Deaffrication—replacement of an affricate sound with a fricative sound *(wash* for *watch)*

- Vocalization—use of a vowel sound in place of a syllabic or postvocalic liquid sound *(zippo* for *zipper)*

The list of phonological processes goals is on page 41. The cross-reference chart for choosing a pattern book by phonological process is on pages 46–47. Children are bombarded with the target phonological pattern as the model story is read. Children have opportunities to use correct production of the target phonological pattern while reading their pattern books.

Articulation Approach—Phonological intervention using a traditional approach to articulation is also possible when using *More Story Making!* Once a child's speech is assessed, *More Story Making!* can be used to remediate specific phonemes, including /s, z, l, r, k, g, ʃ, ʧ, θ, ð, f, v, t, d, n, p, b, m, ʤ/ and semivowels /r, l/. A list of articulation goals is provided on page 41. Once intervention goals are established, a pattern book can be chosen by phoneme using the cross-reference chart for articulation on pages 48–49. Children hear appropriate models of target phonemes as the model story is read. Children have opportunities to correctly produce the target phoneme(s) while reading their pattern books.

Syntax Goals

As children hear the model stories, create their own pattern books, and participate in recommended additional activities, they are exposed to naturally occurring models of syntax. Hearing these targets used in functional, meaningful, and engaging ways allows children to understand their meanings and expand their use.

The syntax goals targeted in the *More Story Making!* books and activities include a variety of early developing grammatical and morphological forms. These goals refer to both comprehension and production of the various linguistic forms. The list of syntax goals is provided on page 42. The cross-reference chart for syntax is on pages 50–51.

Semantics Goals

As children participate in *More Story Making!* activities, they hear and see semantic concepts used in functional, meaningful ways. This helps children learn the meaning of the concepts and provides opportunities for using them.

The semantics goals targeted in the *More Story Making!* books and activities include a variety of early developing concepts of space, time, size, quality, and quantity. These goals refer to both comprehension and production of the various concepts. The list of semantics goals is provided on page 42. The cross-reference chart for semantics is on pages 52–53.

Goals for Thinking Skills

General thinking skills can be heightened as children hear model stories, create their own pattern books, and participate in the additional activities. Goals for thinking skills include making associations, predicting events, establishing causality, making comparisons, drawing inferences, sequencing events or objects, categorizing objects, and detecting and explaining absurdities.

The goals for thinking skills are provided on page 42. The cross-reference chart provided on pages 54–55 makes it easy to choose pattern books based on targeted thinking skills.

Targeting Thematic Learning

A natural outgrowth of literacy experiences and whole language philosophy is thematic teaching to facilitate language learning. A unit is thematic when the "topic or theme is meaningful, relevant to the curriculum and students' lives, consistent with whole language principles, and authentic in the interrelationship of the language processes" (Routman, 1991, p. 278). Themes provide a natural connector that help children integrate old and new information. Children who have less flexible language systems do less networking and generalizing of information than their peers do; therefore thematic learning is more critical to these children (Norris and Hoffman, 1993).

Children need exposure to their world through a variety of formats in an integrated curriculum. Learning materials need to be meaningful so that attention is maintained and optimal learning takes place. Theme teaching allows for organization of information, expansion of preexisting knowledge on a particular topic, reinforcement of target goals, and development of learning strategies. Familiar topics such as people, animals, transportation, time, and places are examples of themes in *More Story Making!* These are themes that are interesting and motivating to young elementary children. The thematic goals are located on page 42.

When collaborating with a classroom teacher, choose model stories that complement current classroom themes. Whenever possible, general curriculum areas such as science, social studies, health, and math should be explored to determine appropriate themes for children. Selecting a topic or theme that is both developmentally appropriate and compatible with the classroom curriculum is important to children's needs and interests. When working with an individual child or small groups of children outside of a collaborative model, choose themes that reflect the interests of the child(ren). A pattern book can be chosen based on themes by using the cross-reference chart provided on pages 56–57.

Targeting Literacy Goals

The objective of *More Story Making!* is to develop children's communication skills. Literacy skills—reading (including phonological awareness) and writing—are seen as critical forms of communication and are targeted through the model stories, the pattern stories, and the additional activities. The literacy goals for phonological awareness, reading, and writing can be found on page 43. Literacy goals are not cross-referenced, since all *More Story Making!* activities support the development of such skills.

General Procedures

More Story Making! presents a process that begins and ends with children immersed in communication and literacy events. Once goals have been determined for each child, the process is initiated by reading popular books (i.e., the model stories) that contain predictable, repetitive language patterns. Children are encouraged to listen and comment during this reading time. As the predictable pattern becomes more familiar to children, they are guided through creating their own stories (i.e., pattern books) using the *More Story Making!* pattern pages provided. The pattern books children create can be shared in class, taken home for further practice, or used as a "launching pad" for related extension activities. Maximum repetition of targeted responses should be the focus of your lessons. Be sure children are proficient with one story before moving on to another.

Consider variables such as the age of the children, size of a group, and length of the sessions when developing lesson plans using the books and activities in *More Story Making!* Use of a model story, creation of its accompanying pattern book, and implementation of at least one additional activity can constitute an entire lesson (approximately 60 minutes) or can be spread out over two or more shorter time periods (e.g., two, 30-minute lessons). The following steps are general guidelines for using *More Story Making!*

1. **Choose a pattern book based on children's goals by using the cross-reference charts.** (See pages 46–57 for cross-reference charts.)

2. **Gather the model story the pattern book is based on.** (Refer to Table 5 on pages 28–31 to find the model story that corresponds to the pattern book.)
   - Model stories used in this resource represent popular children's literature that can be found in most libraries or purchased in bookstores or on the Internet.
   - If a model story cannot be located, use a story that is recommended in the "Additional Activities" section of the story profile, use a similar story, or create and use an enlarged version of the pattern book.

3. Prepare materials.

- Read the story profile related to the pattern book.
- Duplicate pattern pages and illustrations for students to use to create their pattern books (enough copies for each student or group).
- Supply crayons, colored pencils, glue sticks, scissors, pencils, and a stapler.
- Collect items needed to conduct selected additional activities (consider children's goals and amount of time available when selecting activities to use).
- Prepare one customized copy of the *Parent Letter* provided in Appendix D for each child (optional).
- Prepare one customized copy of the *Parent Feedback* form provided in Appendix E for each child (optional).
- Duplicate *Encouraging Literacy Skills at Home* found in Appendix F when first using *More Story Making!* for each child.
- Duplicate one or both of the *Monitoring Progress Form*s from Appendix B for each child and the *Lesson Tracker* from Appendix C for each group.

4. Read the model story.

- Read slowly and expressively using phrasing, pausing, and melodic rise and fall.
- Ask children to repeat all or part of the predictable pattern and to comment on the story as it is read.
- Have children begin to infer and produce the predictable pattern without hearing a model.
- Cue children to complete or say the predictable pattern by supplying words from the pattern if necessary (i.e., use a cloze procedure).
- Continually comment on the content of the model story using targeted language structures (e.g., syntax targets) (i.e., use a scaffolding procedure).
- Help children generate ideas for completion of each predictable pattern as the story goes along (e.g., children can predict what is on the next page); provide phonological or semantic cues to aid students in making reasonable guesses (e.g., if the desired response is the word *pig,* you might say, "The next word starts with the /p/ sound. It is an animal that lives on a farm").

5. **When using *More Story Making!* with children for the first time, make one pattern book together as a group.**
   - Use the children's responses along with their original illustrations or use the illustrations provided.
   - Direct each child to create one or more pattern pages to add to the book.
   - Collate all pages together to make one book (consider enlarging the pattern pages to an 8½" × 11" size, or larger, when creating a book as a group).
   - Place the book in the classroom for children to read.

6. **Have each child make a pattern book.** (See pages 59–62 for procedures on creating pattern books.)

7. **Encourage children to read their pattern books to each other.**
   - Pair children together or have children form small groups to share their stories with each other.
   - Have children read their books to another class of children (e.g., a group of second graders could read their stories to a preschool class).

8. **Conduct one or more additional activities with students.**
   - Additional activities tap into multiple modalities and relate to the targets and/or themes stated in the story profile.
   - Procedures for creating and using interactive language charts, referred to in some of the additional activities, can be found in Appendix H.

9. **Direct children to take their pattern books home to read to family members or caregivers.**
   - Distribute the prepared *Parent Letter*, the prepared *Parent Feedback* form, or both to each child.
   - When using *More Story Making!* with children for the first time, send home *Encouraging Literacy Skills at Home,* provided in Appendix F, for parents to read.

10. **Complete the chosen form(s) for monitoring progress and the form for tracking use of pattern books.**
    - Observe and record students' performance when reading the pattern book and/or participating in additional activities.
    - Track group work using the *Lesson Tracker.*

Adapting Pattern Books

The pattern books and illustrations provided in *More Story Making!* can be adapted in a variety of ways. Be creative and make use of the wealth of stories, activities, and reproducible items. The following are several recommendations:

1. Make a pattern book interactive by using Velcro to attach pictures, words, and pattern pages after the book is laminated. As a pattern book is read, vary how you complete the pattern phrases by varying the pictures and words used on each page.

2. From time to time, create a pattern book with silly responses (e.g., using pictures and words from a different pattern book) and have students talk about what makes each pattern phrase absurd. The *Picture Index* in Appendix G can be used to locate pictures to use from other stories.

3. Use transparency markers or grease pencils to complete the predictable patterns and illustrate the pages after they are laminated. Create a large version of the book as a group or have children create individual books. Show students how they can erase their responses and create a new version of their pattern book story.

4. Create original interactive language charts using the predictable patterns and provided illustrations for any pattern book. Follow the procedures in Appendix H for creating and using interactive language charts.

5. Make specialized picture books using the illustrations provided. The specialized picture books can then be used to provide children with exposure to and practice in specific goal areas. For example, for a group of children who are working on reducing the phonological process of gliding, the following illustrations could be used to make an /r/ book: *raccoon, rat, rock, roadrunner, reindeer, racecar, red [stoplight], wrench, Mount Rushmore,* and *Rocky Mountains).* Select illustrations based on children's goals using the *Picture Index* (see Appendix G). Staple illustrations together to form a small picture book.

6. Create a specialized pattern book using the picture book made during activity #5, by using a rubber stamp that contains a target word (e.g., a

stamp of the word *rock).* Use the stamp on each page of the book and write a corresponding sentence on each page (e.g., *The raccoon is on a rock, The rat is under a rock, There are two rocks).*

7. Use rubber ink stamps or stickers to illustrate pattern pages. Locate stamps or stickers that could logically complete a predictable pattern and have children use these novel materials to create their pattern stories.

8. Conduct memory activities using pattern books. After children have created and become familiar with their books, have them recall the names of the pictures used on each page. Challenge children to recite an entire pattern story if possible.

9. Transfer a *More Story Making!* pattern story (without responses inserted) to a computer using a scanner. Then use a word-processing or desktop-publishing program to have children create versions of their stories on computer. Help students complete the pattern sentences, illustrate their pages, and print out their books.

10. Create original pattern books based on model stories not used in *More Story Making!* Apply the procedures set forth in this resource to turn any children's story into the model story for a pattern book. In addition, refer to *Story Making* (Peura and DeBoer, 1995) for dozens of pattern books and additional activities based on 34 model stories.

11. Create a class pattern book or have pairs or small groups of students create pattern books together to enhance turn taking, problem solving, compromising, and creativity. Have groups read their pattern books to other groups.

Tools for Monitoring Progress

Feedback from *More Story Making!* Sessions

Appendix B provides easy-to-use forms for monitoring progress. These forms can be used to document progress, to track one or more goals for an individual child, or to document performance related to several similar goals for a small group of children.

When using either form from Appendix B, complete it with the child's name, grade, story name(s), and a list of general goal categories (e.g., phonology, semantics). For the generic form, complete the date, list the objective(s), and mark the performance level of each goal for each child, for each session. For the communication rubric, fill in specific objectives for any or all of the stated goals. Write specific targets for each objective under each goal or in the columns that correspond with the child's performance (e.g., under the phonological process goal, *Reduce fronting* and *Reduce final consonant deletion* could be listed as objectives and /k/ could be written in the Inconsistent column, while final /s/ could be written in the Emerging column). For each target listed, date and check the box that corresponds to the child's current level of performance. Store completed forms in each child's file or portfolio and share results with other teachers and/or the child's parent(s).

Feedback from Home

More Story Making! includes a letter to help gather feedback from children's home settings. The *Parent Feedback* form in Appendix E is designed to facilitate correspondence between parents or other caregivers and educators regarding the use of the pattern books at home. The letter is designed to take less than five minutes to complete and can be made specific to each pattern book and to each child's individual goals.

When using this form, complete the date and the goals, and sign each letter before sending home with children. The returned form can be placed in a child's file or portfolio.

Lesson Tracker

The *Lesson Tracker* provided in Appendix C makes it easy to indicate which pattern books have been used with each child or group. Fill in children's names and indicate the date whenever a pattern book is used.

Goals

More Story Making! Goals

The following are lists of goals that can be targeted using *More Story Making!* The goals are broadly stated but can be used to develop objectives with measurable outcomes.

Phonology	
Phonological Processes	**Articulation**
Improve intelligibility of speech by reducing the use of phonological processes.	Improve intelligibility of speech by producing target phonemes /s, z, l, r, k, g, ʃ, tʃ, θ, ð, f, v, t, d, n, p, b, m, dʒ/ and semivowels /r, l/ at the following levels:
1. Reduce assimilation by producing consonant phonemes in correct sequence	1. In isolation
2. Reduce fronting by producing velar phonemes /k, g/	2. In single syllables and words
3. Reduce final consonant deletion by producing final consonant sounds	3. In phrases and sentences
4. Reduce weak syllable deletion by producing unstressed syllables in multisyllabic words	4. While reading
5. Reduce stopping by producing continuant phonemes /f, v, s, z, θ, ð/	5. During structured conversation
6. Reduce gliding by producing liquids /l, r/	6. During spontaneous conversation
7. Reduce cluster simplification by producing consonant /s, r, l, n/ clusters	
8. Reduce depalatalization by producing palatal phonemes /tʃ, ʃ, dʒ/	
9. Reduce deaffrication by producing the affricates /dʒ, tʃ/	
10. Reduce vocalization by producing the syllabic or postvocalic liquids /r, l/ and semivowel /r, l/	

Syntax	Semantics
Comprehend and use the following linguistic structures in obligatory contexts: 1. Forms of negation 2. Verb forms • present tense • present progressive tense • past tense (regular and irregular) • future tense • copula • modal • infinitive • participles 3. Question forms • yes/no • what • who 4. Sentence structures • compound • complex 5. Morphological forms • plurals • articles • noun + *er* 6. Pronouns	Comprehend and use the following basic concepts: 1. Spatial concepts • in • upstairs/downstairs • under/over • through • up/down • around • between • everywhere • on • upside down • backwards 2. Time concepts • morning/night • seasons 3. Quality concepts • descriptors • color 4. Quantity concepts • numbers 5. Size concepts • small/medium/large

Thinking Skills	Themes
1. Make associations 2. Predict events 3. Establish causality 4. Make comparisons 5. Draw inferences 6. Sequence events or objects 7. Categorize objects 8. Detect and explain absurdities	1. Understand new concepts and vocabulary related to a theme by relating them to known information 2. Understand and use new concepts and vocabulary related to a theme in a contrived context 3. Understand and use new concepts and vocabulary related to a theme in new situations

Literacy

Phonological Awareness

1. Identify and produce rhyming and nonrhyming words

2. Segment words in sentences, syllables in words, and phonemes in words

3. Identify initial or final phonemes of words

4. Delete syllables and phonemes from words

5. Blend syllables and phonemes into words

Reading	Writing *
1. Distinguish print from nonprint	1. Use a dominant hand for writing
2. Interact with books appropriately by holding them right-side up, turning pages from right to left, and interacting with text from left to right	2. Write via scribbling
3. Recognize printed symbols	3. Write via drawing
4. Attend to and listen to a story	4. Write letterlike forms
5. Describe what is happening in a story's illustrations	5. Write well-learned units
6. Locate the title and author of a book	6. Use invented spelling
7. Name characters in a story	7. Use conventional spelling
8. Recall words from a patterned sequence of words	8. Use correct spacing for letters and words
9. Listen to and identify rhythmic and rhyming words	9. Use correct capitalization and punctuation
	10. Write basic sentences
	11. Write complex sentences using conjunctions

*These skills are listed hierarchically. Not all children will achieve the highest levels of writing using *More Story Making!*

CROSS-REFERENCE CHARTS

The following cross-reference charts are provided to aid in the selection of *More Story Making!* pattern books. Each pattern book is cross-referenced based on goals for phonology, syntax, semantics, thinking skills, and themes. Multiple goals can be targeted by comparing information across charts.

Phonology Goals
(by phonological process)

Goal	Amanda, Amanda, What Did You Taste?	Animals Should Definitely Not	Blue Spaghetti and Meatballs	The Boat	Bubbles!	A Busy Farm	But Not Like Mine	Carly Bear, What Will You Wear?	Come and Play, Animal Friend!	Come and Play, Creature!	Come and Play, Friend!	A Dark, Dark Cave	Each Pickle Pumpkin Pie	Five Little Monkeys	For Sale	From Here to There	Hannah, Hannah, What Do You Hear?	Hi, Pizza Boy! (Animals)	Hi, Pizza Boy! (Seasonal Characters)	A Hot, Hot Desert	I Am Me! (Dogs)	I Am Me! (People)	I Am Me! (Transportation)	I Like You, Animals
Assimilation								•				•		•						•				
Fronting							•	•	•	•	•	•	•	•	•	•				•				•
FCD		•	•	•	•		•		•	•		•		•		•		•	•	•	•	•	•	
WSD		•	•													•								
Stopping			•	•	•	•								•	•			•	•		•	•	•	•
Gliding		•	•		•		•	•				•	•											•
CS	•		•	•					•	•	•	•	•				•							
Depalatalization		•																						
Deaffrication									•	•	•	•												
Vocalization	•		•	•	•			•				•	•	•		•	•			•				•

FCD=Final Consonant Deletion   WSD=Weak Syllable Deletion   CS=Cluster Simplification

Phonology Goals—*Continued*
(by phonological process)

Goal	I Like You, Colors	Itchy, Itchy Mosquito Bites!	I Think I Can, I Think I Can! (Chores)	I Think I Can, I Think I Can! (Sports)	It's Not Safe!	I've Been Working at My School	I've Been Working on My House	Jolly Joshua	Kid's Day	My Pet Cat	My Pet Dog	One Bright Fall Morning	A-Riding We Will Go	A-Shopping We Will Go	Showy Shelly	The Sled	Stanley Gets Ready for School!	Time for Spring!	To the Zoo We'll Go	The Very Hungry Bear	What Moves in the Forest at Night?	Who Walks in the Zoo at Night?	Zicka Zicka Zoom Zoom!
Assimilation			•	•						•	•												•
Fronting	•		•	•		•	•		•				•	•			•		•				•
FCD			•	•		•	•	•		•	•				•	•	•			•	•	•	•
WSD																							•
Stopping	•	•	•	•	•				•				•	•		•	•	•	•		•	•	•
Gliding	•		•										•	•			•		•	•			•
CS		•		•					•	•	•	•				•	•	•			•	•	•
Depalatalization								•					•	•	•			•					•
Deaffrication		•						•						•									•
Vocalization	•					•	•	•	•			•	•	•			•		•	•	•		•

FCD=Final Consonant Deletion   WSD=Weak Syllable Deletion   CS=Cluster Simplification

Phonology Goals
(by phoneme)

Goal	Amanda, Amanda, What Did You Taste?	Animals Should Definitely Not	Blue Spaghetti and Meatballs	The Boat	Bubbles!	A Busy Farm	But Not Like Mine	Carly Bear, What Will You Wear?	Come and Play, Animal Friend!	Come and Play, Creature!	Come and Play, Friend!	A Dark, Dark Cave	Each Pickle Pumpkin Pie	Five Little Monkeys	For Sale	From Here to There	Hannah, Hannah, What Do You Hear?	Hi, Pizza Boy! (Animals)	Hi, Pizza Boy! (Seasonal Characters)	A Hot, Hot Desert	I Am Me! (Dogs)	I Am Me! (People)	I Am Me! (Transportation)	I Like You, Animals
/s/ and /z/	•		•	•	•	•	•							•	•		•	•	•		•	•	•	
/l/ and semivowel /l/		•	•		•		•	•	•	•		•	•			•								•
/r/ and semivowel /r/	•			•		•		•	•	•	•	•	•	•		•	•		•					•
/k/ and /g/			•				•	•	•	•	•	•	•	•	•	•				•				•
/θ/ and /ð/						•			•	•	•	•								•				
/f/ and /v/						•						•		•	•			•	•	•				•
/ʃ/		•																						
/tʃ/								•	•	•		•	•											
/p/, /b/, and /m/			•	•	•		•		•	•	•		•	•				•			•	•	•	
/d/, /t/, and /n/	•	•	•	•	•		•					•					•	•	•	•				
/ʤ/																								

Phonology Goals—*Continued*
(by phoneme)

Goal	I Like You, Colors	Itchy, Itchy Mosquito Bites!	I Think I Can, I Think I Can! (Chores)	I Think I Can, I Think I Can! (Sports)	It's Not Safe!	I've Been Working at My School	I've Been Working on My House	Jolly Joshua	Kid's Day	My Pet Cat	My Pet Dog	One Bright Fall Morning	A-Riding We Will Go	A-Shopping We Will Go	Showy Shelly	The Sled	Stanley Gets Ready for School!	Time for Spring!	To the Zoo We'll Go	The Very Hungry Bear	What Moves in the Forest at Night?	Who Walks in the Zoo at Night?	Zicka Zicka Zoom Zoom!
/s/ and /z/		•			•	•	•		•	•	•	•	•	•		•	•	•	•		•	•	•
/l/ and semivowel /l/	•				•			•	•				•	•	•		•	•	•	•			•
/r/ and semivowel /r/	•		•		•	•	•		•	•	•	•	•	•		•	•	•	•				•
/k/ and /g/	•		•	•		•	•	•	•	•	•		•	•			•		•				•
/θ/ and /ð/			•	•		•	•		•				•				•		•				•
/f/ and /v/	•				•												•	•			•	•	•
/ʃ/								•					•	•	•					•			•
/tʃ/		•																		•			•
/p/, /b/, and /m/		•						•	•					•	•					•			•
/d/, /t/, and /n/			•	•	•			•						•	•	•				•	•	•	•
/dʒ/								•							•								•

49

More Story Making!

Syntax																								
Goal / Pattern Book	Amanda, Amanda, What Did You Taste?	Animals Should Definitely Not	Blue Spaghetti and Meatballs	The Boat	Bubbles!	A Busy Farm	But Not Like Mine	Carly Bear, What Will You Wear?	Come and Play, Animal Friend!	Come and Play, Creature!	Come and Play, Friend!	A Dark, Dark Cave	Each Pickle Pumpkin Pie	Five Little Monkeys	For Sale	From Here to There	Hannah, Hannah, What Do You Hear?	Hi, Pizza Boy! (Animals)	Hi, Pizza Boy! (Seasonal Characters)	A Hot, Hot Desert	I Am Me! (Dogs)	I Am Me! (People)	I Am Me! (Transportation)	I Like You, Animals
Negation		•	•				•											•	•					
Verb Forms																								
present	•		•	•		•			•	•	•		•		•		•							
present progressive						•								•										
past	•			•													•							
future								•										•	•					
copula						•						•			•			•	•	•	•	•	•	•
modal	•	•											•		•	•	•							•
participle						•																		
irregular past														•										
infinitive	•																•							
Question Forms																								
yes/no													•			•								
what	•						•										•	•						
who																								
Sentence Structures																								
compound																•		•						
complex		•					•	•		•	•	•	•							•	•	•		•
Morphological Forms																								
plurals	•					•			•					•		•								
articles	•	•			•	•	•	•	•	•	•	•	•		•	•	•	•	•	•	•	•	•	•
possessives			•				•		•	•	•		•	•										
noun + er																•								
Pronouns	•		•				•	•	•	•	•		•			•	•	•			•	•	•	•

50

Goal	I Like You, Colors	Itchy, Itchy Mosquito Bites!	I Think I Can, I Think I Can! (Chores)	I Think I Can, I Think I Can! (Sports)	It's Not Safe!	I've Been Working at My School	I've Been Working on My House	Jolly Joshua	Kid's Day	My Pet Cat	My Pet Dog	One Bright Fall Morning	A-Riding We Will Go	A-Shopping We Will Go	Showy Shelly	The Sled	Stanley Gets Ready for School!	Time for Spring!	To the Zoo We'll Go	The Very Hungry Bear	What Moves in the Forest at Night?	Who Walks in the Zoo at Night?	Zicka Zicka Zoom Zoom!
Negation			•	•	•																		
Verb Forms																							
present		•	•	•						•	•					•		•			•	•	•
present progressive													•	•				•					
past						•	•		•														
future													•	•				•					•
copula	•				•					•	•	•	•	•				•					
modal	•		•	•												•							
participle						•	•					•									•	•	
irregular past									•			•			•		•			•			
infinitive										•	•						•				•	•	
Question Forms																							
yes/no																	•						•
what																	•						
who																					•	•	
Sentence Structures																							
compound			•	•									•	•				•	•	•			
complex	•									•		•											
Morphological Forms																							
plurals		•				•	•			•	•	•					•			•			
articles	•				•	•	•			•	•		•	•	•	•	•			•	•	•	•
possessives		•				•	•			•	•												
noun + er																							
Pronouns	•	•	•	•	•	•	•	•	•	•	•	•	•	•	•	•	•	•	•	•			

51

Goal	Amanda, Amanda, What Did You Taste?	Animals Should Definitely Not	Blue Spaghetti and Meatballs	The Boat	Bubbles!	A Busy Farm	But Not Like Mine	Carly Bear, What Will You Wear?	Come and Play, Animal Friend!	Come and Play, Creature!	Come and Play, Friend!	A Dark, Dark Cave	Each Pickle Pumpkin Pie	Five Little Monkeys	For Sale	From Here to There	Hannah, Hannah, What Do You Hear?	Hi, Pizza Boy! (Animals)	Hi, Pizza Boy! (Seasonal Characters)	A Hot, Hot Desert	I Am Me! (Dogs)	I Am Me! (People)	I Am Me! (Transportation)	I Like You, Animals
Spatial Concepts																								
above/below																								
around					•																			
between			•																					
beside/next to			•																					
in/out		•	•	•								•	•	•						•				
inside/outside																								
on		•			•	•							•	•										
over/under			•											•										
up/down			•		•								•	•										
upside down																								
everywhere																								
backwards																								
Time Concepts																								
morning/night																								
days of the week																								
seasons			•					•																
Quality Concepts																								
size				•	•		•								•									
colors		•													•									•
descriptors	•						•		•	•	•	•	•				•	•	•	•	•	•	•	
Quantity Concepts																								
numbers									•	•	•			•										

52

Goal	I Like You, Colors	Itchy, Itchy Mosquito Bites!	I Think I Can, I Think I Can! (Chores)	I Think I Can, I Think I Can! (Sports)	It's Not Safe!	I've Been Working at My School	I've Been Working on My House	Jolly Joshua	Kid's Day	My Pet Cat	My Pet Dog	One Bright Fall Morning	A-Riding We Will Go	A-Shopping We Will Go	Showy Shelly	The Sled	Stanley Gets Ready for School!	Time for Spring!	To the Zoo We'll Go	The Very Hungry Bear	What Moves in the Forest at Night?	Who Walks in the Zoo at Night?	Zicka Zicka Zoom Zoom!
Semantics—*Continued*																							
Spatial Concepts																							
above/below													•	•					•				
around																							
between																							
beside/next to																							
in/out													•	•		•			•		•	•	
inside/outside																							
on		•								•	•					•							
over/under													•	•					•				
up/down																	•						•
upside down									•						•								
everywhere										•													
backwards								•							•								
Time Concepts																							
morning/night																	•				•	•	
days of the week												•											
seasons																		•	•				
Quality Concepts																							
size																•							
colors	•																						
descriptors										•	•	•									•	•	
Quantity Concepts																							
numbers		•										•							•				

Thinking Skills

Goal	Amanda, Amanda, What Did You Taste?	Animals Should Definitely Not	Blue Spaghetti and Meatballs	The Boat	Bubbles!	A Busy Farm	But Not Like Mine	Carly Bear, What Will You Wear?	Come and Play, Animal Friend	Come and Play, Creature!	Come and Play, Friend!	A Dark, Dark Cave!	Each Pickle Pumpkin Pie	Five Little Monkeys	For Sale	From Here to There	Hannah, Hannah, What Do You Hear?	Hi, Pizza Boy! (Animals)	Hi, Pizza Boy! (Seasonal Characters)	A Hot, Hot Desert	I Am Me! (Dogs)	I Am Me! (People)	I Am Me! (Transportation)	I Like You, Animals
Associations	•	•				•		•	•	•	•	•		•		•	•	•	•	•	•	•	•	•
Predictions	•				•												•	•	•					
Causality				•		•		•																
Comparisons		•	•	•			•							•							•	•	•	
Inferencing									•	•	•							•	•					•
Sequencing					•								•											
Categorization			•					•			•		•							•				
Absurdities		•	•						•	•	•													

54

Thinking Skills—*Continued*

Goal	I Like You, Colors	Itchy, Itchy Mosquito Bites!	I Think I Can, I Think I Can! (Chores)	I Think I Can, I Think I Can! (Sports)	It's Not Safe!	I've Been Working at My School	I've Been Working on My House	Jolly Joshua	Kid's Day	My Pet Cat	My Pet Dog	One Bright Fall Morning	A-Riding We Will Go	A-Shopping We Will Go	Showy Shelly	The Sled	Stanley Gets Ready for School!	Time for Spring!	To the Zoo We'll Go	The Very Hungry Bear	What Moves in the Forest at Night?	Who Walks in the Zoo at Night?	Zicka Zicka Zoom Zoom!
Associations	•					•	•		•	•	•							•					•
Predictions					•			•				•			•		•	•		•			•
Causality		•			•				•							•	•	•		•			
Comparisons			•	•												•							
Inferencing	•		•	•						•	•	•											
Sequencing		•										•	•	•				•	•	•			
Categorization						•	•		•				•	•		•			•		•	•	
Absurdities								•						•									

Theme	Amanda, Amanda, What Did You Taste?	Animals Should Definitely Not	Blue Spaghetti and Meatballs	The Boat	Bubbles!	A Busy Farm	But Not Like Mine	Carly Bear, What Will You Wear?	Come and Play, Animal Friend!	Come and Play, Creature!	Come and Play, Friend!	A Dark, Dark Cave	Each Pickle Pumpkin Pie	Five Little Monkeys	For Sale	From Here to There	Hannah, Hannah, What Do You Hear?	Hi, Pizza Boy! (Animals)	Hi, Pizza Boy! (Seasonal Characters)	A Hot, Hot Desert	I Am Me! (Dogs)	I Am Me! (People)	I Am Me! (Transportation)	I Like You, Animals
Actions	•					•								•		•	•							
Animals		•		•	•	•	•		•	•	•							•	•		•	•	•	•
Body Parts	•				•				•	•	•						•							
Clothing								•										•	•					
Colors			•											•										•
Counting													•	•										
Food	•		•																•					
Imagination		•	•						•	•	•													
Nature							•					•								•				
People		•					•		•	•	•					•		•	•		•	•	•	
Places												•								•				•
Rhymes					•								•											
School														•										
Time				•				•										•	•					
Toys																								
Transportation																					•	•	•	

	Themes—*Continued*																						
Theme \ **Pattern Book**	*I Like You, Colors*	*Itchy, Itchy Mosquito Bites!*	*I Think I Can, I Think I Can! (Chores)*	*I Think I Can, I Think I Can! (Sports)*	*It's Not Safe!*	*I've Been Working at My School*	*I've Been Working on My House*	*Jolly Joshua*	*Kid's Day*	*My Pet Cat*	*My Pet Dog*	*One Bright Fall Morning*	*A-Riding We Will Go*	*A-Shopping We Will Go*	*Showy Shelly*	*The Sled*	*Stanley Gets Ready for School!*	*Time for Spring!*	*To the Zoo We'll Go*	*The Very Hungry Bear*	*What Moves in the Forest at Night?*	*Who Walks in the Zoo at Night?*	*Zicka Zicka Zoom Zoom!*
Actions			●	●	●	●	●			●	●							●					
Animals	●									●	●		●	●		●		●	●	●	●	●	●
Body Parts		●																					
Clothing																							
Colors	●																						
Counting		●										●								●			
Food																				●			
Imagination																							●
Nature												●						●					
People								●							●								
Places	●							●					●	●	●				●				
Rhymes										●	●		●	●						●		●	●
School						●	●		●								●						●
Time												●				●		●					
Toys									●														
Transportation													●	●					●				

More Story Making! Pattern Books

Instructions

Each *More Story Making!* book consists of several pages of patterns and illustrations. Below are step-by-step directions for creating a *More Story Making!* pattern book. The directions assume that each child will be creating his or her own pattern book. Make necessary adaptations when small or large groups are constructing a single book cooperatively. Note that a story profile always precedes the pattern book pages and illustrations. More specific information about the contents and usefulness of the story profiles can be found on page 62.

1. Make one copy of the title page and the final page for each child. Make several copies of the pages containing the predictable pattern for the story. The number of pages for each child's pattern book can vary, depending on each child's goals and attention span. For a few books, the number of pattern pages is dictated by the story. Cut all pages in half.

2. Choose from the following illustration options:

   - Copy and cut out the illustrations and captions provided in *More Story Making!*
   - Have children illustrate pages with their own drawings.
   - Have children use pictures cut from catalogs or magazines.
   - Ask children to bring in photographs from home.

   The number of illustrations needed will depend on the number of pattern pages in each book. Have children choose their own responses unless specific responses are needed to achieve established goals (e.g., having a child use illustrations for which the target words contain /r/ when working on generalization of /r/ into the predictable pattern).

3. Give each child the title page, the final page, the pattern pages, and the set of illustrations (unless children are creating their own art, cutting pictures from magazines or catalogs, or bringing in photographs from home). Provide scissors and a glue stick for children to use with the illustrations.

4. Have children write their name on the title page.

5. Direct children to cut around each illustration rather than cutting on the lines of each illustration. (Making a thick line around the illustrations prior to photocopying can help younger children.) If necessary, cut out the illustrations before meeting with children. Children should then glue each illustration onto a pattern page.

6. Guide children as they complete each predictable pattern. Younger children can dictate their responses for an adult to write in the blanks. Older children can write their own responses or copy the response from the model provided below each illustration. As another option, children can cut out the words above and below the pictures and glue them on the corresponding blank lines.

7. Have children draw a picture on the final page of their book. The "Notes" section on the first page of each story profile provides suggestions about what children might draw on these pages.

8. When children have completed their pattern book, staple each book together or bind it with string or yarn. Have children color their illustrations as they wish. If time permits, children could color their illustrations prior to gluing them onto each pattern page.

9. Provide several opportunities for each child to read or tell his or her created storybook. Encourage children to read their stories to each other, to siblings, and to parents or other caregivers.

Sample *More Story Making!* Pattern Book

Figure 1 is an example of a completed *More Story Making!* pattern book. The pattern book contains a title page, which includes the name of the pattern book and the child's name as the author. Following the title page, the pattern

Figure 1   ***More Story Making!* Pattern Book Example**

title page

Hi,
Pizza Boy!

by ___Jack___

page 2
of the book

What if it's not a pizza boy? What if it's a

pizza ___pig___ . Then what will you say?
(animal)

___Oink___ , ___Oink___ , pizza ___pig___ !
(animal sound)   (animal sound)   (animal)

cut-out illustration from
More Story Making!

one of child's handwritten
pattern phrase responses

pages contain the illustrations with the predictable patterns filled in. In the example, the child chose an illustration provided in *More Story Making!*, glued it onto the pattern page, and filled in the words to complete the predictable patterns. The final page to the pattern book is not shown in Figure 1, but would include an original illustration created by the child.

About the Story Profiles

The *More Story Making!* pattern pages are preceded by a story profile designed to assist educators in choosing a pattern book that targets specific skills. The story profiles are merely a starting point for the educator's creativity; they should not be considered the only options for enhancing learning through *More Story Making!*

Each story profile provides bibliographic information for the model story. The predictable pattern for the pattern story is also listed in each story profile. This language pattern is always the basis for the pattern books created by students. Children hear the language pattern in the model story first, then hear it and say it again and again as they make and read their own books.

Most story profiles give directions for creating a single pattern book, but several give directions for two or three pattern books. The "Notes" section in each story profile includes specific directions for constructing the corresponding pattern book(s).

Goals for phonology, syntax, semantics, and thinking skills are listed in each story profile. These goals are simply suggestions and are not meant to limit the possible uses for the pattern books. Following the goals, the general themes of the story are stated.

Finally, each story profile suggests additional activities that complement the pattern book(s). Among these suggestions are additional books to read, language experience activities, activities to develop thinking skills (including multiple intelligence activities and memory training), phonological awareness activities appropriate for large classrooms or small groups, and creative arts-and-crafts activities designed to stimulate learning. Educators are encouraged to be creative and feel free to develop customized goals and activities while using *More Story Making!*

STORY PROFILE

Animals Should Definitely Not

Model Story: ***Animals Should Definitely Not Act Like People***
(1989)
by Judi Barrett
New York: Aladdin

Description: This 31-page book depicts the inconveniences animals would be burdened with if they behaved like people.

Predictable Pattern: Animals should definitely not act like people, because

_____ would _____.
        (animal)   (action)

Notes: Children should complete the predictable pattern with the reason why the pictured animal should not do the action shown (e.g., a goat should not *mow* the lawn, because a goat would *eat* the grass). The final page is on the bottom half of page 66. Have children use that page to draw a person acting like a particular animal and to supply the reason the person should not do the action drawn (e.g., people should definitely not act like animals, because a person would get all dirty if it took a bath like a pig).

Goals: 1. *Phonology*
Reduce final consonant deletion (FCD)
Reduce weak syllable deletion (WSD)
Reduce gliding
Reduce depalatalization
Produce /ʃ/
Produce /t/

Produce /d/

Produce /l/

2. *Syntax*

Comprehend and use forms of negation

Comprehend and use verb forms (modal)

Comprehend and use sentence structure (complex)

Comprehend and use morphological forms (articles)

3. *Semantics*

Comprehend and use spatial concepts (on, in)

4. *Thinking Skills*

Make associations

Make comparisons

Detect and explain absurdities

Themes: People

Animals

Imagination

Additional Activities: 1. Read additional books:

Dogs Don't Wear Sneakers (1996)

by Laura Numeroff

New York: Aladdin

Description: This imaginative rhyming book has animals doing unusual activities.

Animals Should Definitely Not Wear Clothing

(1989)

by Judi Barrett

New York: Aladdin

Description: This book shows how silly it would be for animals to wear clothing.

Silly Willy (1995)

by Maryann Cocca-Leffler

New York: Grosset and Dunlap

Description: As Silly Willy gets dressed, he puts his clothing on the wrong body parts, reminding his mother of various animals. This story uses simple words and rebus pictures.

2. Draw children's attention to each illustration in the model storybook. Talk about the reasons why the animals would not do the pictured actions.

3. Find pictures that contain absurdities, such as magazine ads. Show the pictures to children and have them tell what they see and why it is strange.

4. Locate pictures of various animals, such as those on pages 86–87. Photocopy the pictures and cut them in half. Pair up mismatching animal tops and bottoms and tape the pieces together. Talk about how silly the combinations look. Help students make up names and descriptions for the animal creations (e.g., a bird top and raccoon bottom could be a *bircoon;* a beaver top with rabbit feet could be a *beebit)*.

5. Enlarge a copy of the sentences from the model story and create strips that can be used with a pocket chart. Have students count and clap out the number of words in the predictable pattern as you point to each word.

Animals Should Definitely Not

by _____

People should definitely not act like animals, because a person would _____.

(action)

66

Animals should definitely not act like people, because _____ would _____.
(animal)   (action)

Animals should definitely not act like people, because _____ would _____.
(animal)   (action)

© 2000 Thinking Publications

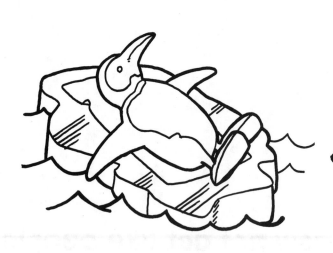

a penguin

a bird

an elephant

a skunk

a goat

a moose

a cow

a kangaroo

69

© 2000 Thinking Publications

STORY PROFILE

Blue Spaghetti and Meatballs

Model Story: *Green Eggs and Ham* (1960)
by Dr. Seuss
New York: Random House

Description: In this 62-page book, Sam-I-Am attempts to get a cat to eat green eggs and ham in a variety of places.

Predictable Pattern: I do not like blue spaghetti and meatballs. I do not like it _____.
(place)

Notes: Children should complete the predictable pattern with different places they might eat spaghetti and meatballs. The final page is on the bottom half of page 73. Use that page to have children draw either a food or an activity they might like to try.

Goals: 1. *Phonology*
Reduce final consonant deletion (FCD)
Reduce stopping
Reduce gliding
Reduce weak syllable deletion (WSD)
Reduce cluster simplification (CS)
Produce /s/ and /z/
Produce /l/
Produce /b/ and /m/
Produce /k/
Produce /d/, /t/, and /n/

2. *Syntax*
Comprehend and use forms of negation

Comprehend and use verb forms (present)

Comprehend and use pronouns

3. *Semantics*

Comprehend and use spatial concepts
   (in, under, over, up, down, between, beside)

Comprehend and use quality concepts (colors)

4. *Thinking Skills*

Make comparisons

Detect and explain absurdities

Themes: Colors

Food

Imagination

Additional Activities: 1. Read additional books:

The Cat in the Hat (1957)
by Dr. Seuss
New York: Random House

Description: The Cat in the Hat transforms a dull, rainy afternoon into a magical and messy adventure.

One Fish, Two Fish, Red Fish, Blue Fish (1981)
by Dr. Seuss
New York: Random House

Description: This book is a story-poem about the activities of such unusual animals as Nooks, Wumps, Yinks, Yops, Gaps, and Zeds.

2. Use food coloring to make green eggs and ham or blue spaghetti and meatballs. Have children compare their taste and visual appeal to that of traditional servings of the same foods. This could also be done with other foods (e.g., blue ice cream and white ice cream, red bread and white bread). Make a list of children's likes and dislikes as they taste

the different foods. Take pictures of the children's expressions as they are taste-testing.

3. Play a preposition game using one or more plates and several pictures of food items. Have children follow a variety of directions (e.g., "Put the food under a plate; Put the food between two plates; Put the food beside a plate"). Then, have children take turns giving directions to a partner.

4. Make a macaroni necklace. Place macaroni in a Ziploc bag. Pour rubbing alcohol into bag and work into macaroni until each piece is covered (be careful not to use too much rubbing alcohol). Place several drops of food coloring into bag and work into macaroni until each piece is coated. Let macaroni dry at least 24 hours. Have children string the colored macaroni together with yarn or string. Children can copy a given color pattern or create their own patterns. Have children describe their patterns when their necklaces are complete.

Blue Spaghetti and Meatballs

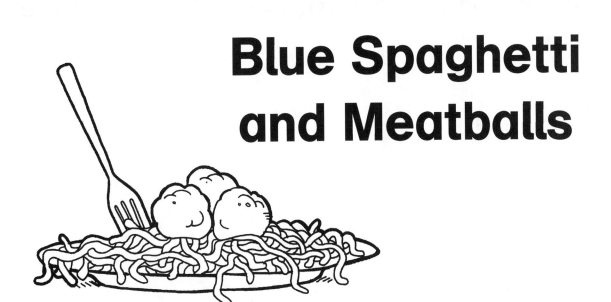

by _____

If I try something new, I just might like it!

I do not like blue spaghetti and meatballs.

I do not like it _____.
(place)

I do not like blue spaghetti and meatballs.

I do not like it _____.
(place)

74

in a car

under a bridge

up in a tree

over a cloud

75

© 2000 Thinking Publications

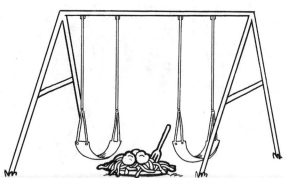

between two swings

down in a hole

with a book

beside a river

STORY PROFILES

The Boat
The Sled

Model Story: *The Mitten* (1996)
adapted and illustrated by Jan Brett
New York: Putnam

Description: In this 32-page story, a boy loses his snow-white mitten in the snow. Woodland animals find it and try to squeeze inside the mitten.

Predictable Patterns:

The Boat: The _____ squeezes into the boat.
　　　　　　　　　(animal)

The Sled: The _____ squeezes onto the sled.
　　　　　　　　　(animal)

Notes: Two different pattern books are provided. Children should complete either predictable pattern with an animal name. For *The Boat,* the title page and final page are on page 80, the pattern pages are on page 81, and the illustrations are on pages 82–83. Children can draw a picture of all the animals falling out of the boat on the final page.

For *The Sled,* the title page and final page are on page 84, the pattern pages are on page 85, and the illustrations are on pages 86–87. Children can draw a picture of all the animals falling off the sled on the final page.

Goals: 1. *Phonology*
Reduce stopping
Reduce vocalization

Reduce cluster simplification (CS)

Reduce final consonant deletion (FCD)

Produce /s/ and /z/

Produce /t/ and /d/

Produce /b/

Produce semivowel /r/

2. *Syntax*

Comprehend and use verb forms (present)

Comprehend and use morphological forms (articles)

3. *Semantics*

Comprehend and use spatial concepts (in[to], on[to])

Comprehend and use time concepts (seasons)

Comprehend and use quality concepts (size)

4. *Thinking Skills*

Make comparisons

Establish causality

Categorize objects

Themes: Animals

Time (seasons)

Additional Activities:

1. Read an additional book:

The Hat (1999)

by Jan Brett

New York: Putnam

Description: After getting his nose stuck in a wool stocking, Hedgie is teased by all the other farm animals. Hedgie gets the last laugh when all the other farm animals start wearing things on their heads.

2. Categorize objects or pictures associated with winter and objects or pictures associated with summer. Then categorize pictures of animals associated with the water and animals associated with the

forest. Pictures provided on pages 82–83 and 86–87 can be used.

3. Locate several different containers and fill them with objects (e.g., marbles, pennies, animal crackers). Have children predict the number of objects that are in each container. After everyone has guessed, have children help count the objects to find the actual answer.

4. Count the number of animals that squeezed into the boat or onto the sled in each child's story.

5. Place snow in a sensory table or in a large tub and let children play with it. Have them comment about the changes they observe as the snow melts. Describe the similarities and differences between snow and water.

The Boat

by _____

I don't think we all fit in the boat on the water!

The

_____

(animal)

squeezes into

the boat.

The

_____

(animal)

squeezes into

the boat.

© 2000 Thinking Publications

whale

dolphin

seal

lobster

sea horse

crab

octopus

fish

83

© 2000 Thinking Publications

The Sled

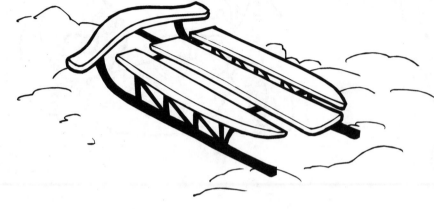

by _____

I don't think we all fit on the sled in the snow!

84

The

_____

(animal)

squeezes onto

the sled.

The

_____

(animal)

squeezes onto

the sled.

bear

deer

bird

raccoon

elk

beaver

wolf

rabbit

87

STORY PROFILE

Bubbles!

Model Story: None

Description: In this pattern book developed by Robin Peura-Jones, children recite a rhyme while blowing bubbles onto a variety of objects and/or pictures.

Predictable Pattern:
Bubbles, bubbles up and down.
Bubbles, bubbles all around.
Some just landed on my _____.
                                   (object)

Pop! Pop! Pop!

Notes: Children should blow bubbles while making this pattern book. Each time a bubble lands on something, the corresponding word can be used to complete the predictable pattern. Children can draw what the bubbles land on or use the pictures provided on pages 93–98 to complete the pattern pages. Pictures for rhyming objects, body parts, and a variety of bears are provided. The final page appears on the bottom half of page 91. Children can draw small, medium, and large bubbles on that page.

Goals: 1. *Phonology*
Reduce final consonant deletion (FCD)
Reduce vocalization
Reduce stopping
Reduce gliding
Produce /b/ and /p/
Produce /n/ and /d/

Produce /s/ and /z/
Produce /l/

2. *Syntax*
Comprehend and use verb forms (past)
Comprehend and use morphological forms
(plurals, possessives)

3. *Semantics*
Comprehend and use spatial concepts
(on, up, down, around)
Comprehend and use quality concepts (size)

4. *Thinking Skills*
Predict events
Sequence events or objects

Themes: Body parts
Animals (bears)
Rhymes

Additional
Activities: 1. Read an additional book:
Bubble Trouble (1995)
by Mary Packard
New York: Scholastic

Description: A fun-filled day of bubbles in the tub,
in the sink, and in the air is presented
in a vocabulary-building, rhyming
text.

2. Make bubble pictures by blowing bubbles toward
a piece of colored paper. Children can describe
the sizes of the bubbles while making their pictures.

3. When using rhyming words to complete a pattern
story, categorize the words by their rhyme families
(e.g., *-at, -og)*. Talk about how all the words that complete the predictable pattern have the same ending.

4. Create an interactive language chart using the sentences in the framed box below. Refer to the procedures provided in Appendix H (page 379) for creating and using an interactive language chart.

> Bubbles, bubbles up and down.
>
> Bubbles, bubbles all around.
>
> Some just landed on my _____.
>
> Pop! Pop! Pop!

Bubbles!

by _____

**I can make small bubbles,
medium bubbles, and large bubbles!**

© 2000 Thinking Publications

Bubbles, bubbles up and down.

Bubbles, bubbles all around.

Some just landed on

my _____.

(object)

Pop! Pop! Pop!

Bubbles, bubbles up and down.

Bubbles, bubbles all around.

Some just landed on

my _____.

(object)

Pop! Pop! Pop!

cat

hat

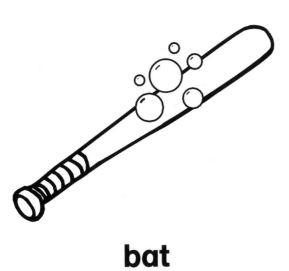

bat

rat

93

hog

dog

log

frog

hand

head

foot

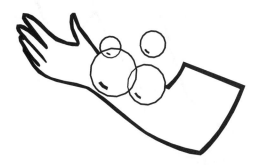

arm

leg

back

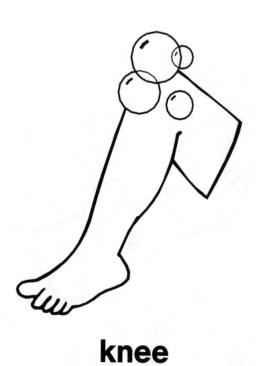

knee

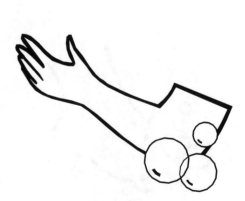

elbow

koala bear

black bear

polar bear

brown bear

grizzly bear

bear cub

panda bear

teddy bear

98

STORY PROFILE

A Busy Farm

Model Story: *The Napping House* (1984)
by Audrey Wood
New York: Harcourt Brace

Description: In this 32-page cumulative tale, a wakeful flea atop a number of sleeping creatures causes a commotion with just one bite.

Predictable Pattern: There is a _____ _____ on a
                                                 (action)   (animal)

busy farm, where everyone is moving.

Notes: The predictable pattern should be completed with an animal's name and its characteristic action. The final page is on the bottom half of page 101. Children can draw animals resting or sleeping on that page.

Goals: 1. *Phonology*
Reduce stopping
Reduce vocalization
Produce /f/ and /v/
Produce semivowel /r/
Produce /θ/
Produce /z/

2. *Syntax*
Comprehend and use verb forms
    (present, copula, participle, present progressive)
Comprehend and use sentence structures (complex)
Comprehend and use morphological forms (articles)

3. *Thinking Skills*
   Make associations
   Establish causality

Themes: Animals (farm)
Actions

Additional Activities:

1. Read an additional book:
   Inside a Barn in the Country (1995)
   by Alyssa Satin Capcilli
   New York: Scholastic

   Description: In this cumulative tale, a squeaky mouse causes a commotion that wakes up the farm animals. The book is a rebus, read-along story.

2. Duplicate an additional set of the animal pictures on pages 103–104. Help children sequence the farm animals according to their actual sizes, from smallest to largest.

3. Investigate body movements with children. Have children move around in different ways (e.g., waddling, galloping, jumping with both feet, hopping on one foot, skipping, prancing, and walking) and talk about the animal who might do that action.

4. Present pictures of pets, zoo animals, and farm animals. Have children sort the animals into these three categories.

5. Have children come up with a rhyming word (real or nonsensical) for each animal that appears in their pattern book.

A Busy Farm

by _____

This is a tired farm now, where
everyone is resting.

There is a

_____

(action)

_____

(animal)

on a busy farm, where everyone is moving.

There is a

_____

(action)

_____

(animal)

on a busy farm, where everyone is moving.

galloping horse

jumping frog

running goat

swimming fish

103

© 2000 Thinking Publications

flying bird

waddling duck

charging bull

walking cow

STORY PROFILE

But Not Like Mine

Model Story: *But Not Like Mine* (1988)
by Margery Facklam
New York: Harcourt Brace

Description: This 20-page book uses fold-back pages to help children discover that some animals have body parts that are similar to human body parts.

Predictable Pattern: _____ has _____ for a
                     (animal or person)   (type of home)
home, but not like mine.

Notes: A book can be created for animal homes, human homes, or both. Have children complete the pattern with an animal or person name and the corresponding home. The final page of the book is on the bottom half of page 107. Children can draw their own homes on that page.

Goals: 1. *Phonology*
Reduce final consonant deletion (FCD)
Reduce gliding
Reduce fronting
Produce /z/
Produce /l/
Produce /k/
Produce /t/
Produce /m/

2. *Syntax*
Comprehend and use negation
Comprehend and use sentence structures (complex)
Comprehend and use morphological forms
    (possessives, articles)
Comprehend and use pronouns

3. *Semantics*

Comprehend and use quality concepts
(size, descriptors)

4. *Thinking Skill*

Make comparisons

Themes: Animals

Nature

People

Additional Activities:

1. Read an additional book:

A House Is a House for Me (1982)
by Mary Ann Hoberman
New York: Viking

Description: This rhyming book describes the homes of animals and humans.

2. Create animal flip books using pictures of four-legged animals. For each book, gather several animal pictures of the same size and same orientation (i.e., all standing horizontally or all standing vertically) and stack the pictures. Staple along one edge of the stack (top edge for animals standing horizontally and side edge for animals standing vertically). Make two cuts through each stack, starting at the edge opposite the staples and ending just before the staples, separating the heads, bodies, and rears of the animals. Have children flip the pages of their books to make silly composite pictures (e.g., the head of a tiger, the body of a cow, and the rear of a zebra). Have children describe and name their silly combinations.

3. Divide a large piece of construction paper into four rectangles by folding it or drawing lines. Have students draw one place where they have lived or visited in each rectangle and describe their pictures to each other.

But Not Like Mine

by _____

Nobody has a special home like mine!

_____
(animal or person)

has

_____
(type of home)

for a home,
but not like mine.

_____
(animal or person)

has

_____
(type of home)

for a home,
but not like mine.

A bear

An ant

A bee

A mole

109

An eagle

A dolphin

A crab

A joey

110

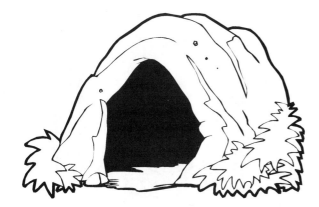

a cave

a hill

a hive

a tunnel

© 2000 Thinking Publications

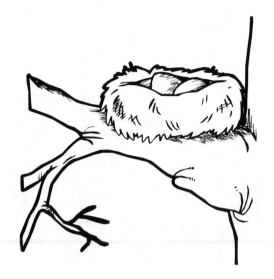

a nest

an ocean

a shell

a pouch

A camper

A rock star

A sailor

A hiker

113

A Pilgrim

An island dweller

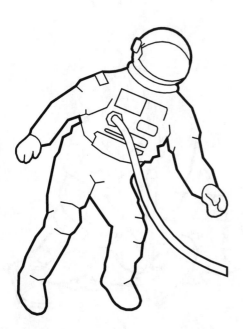

An astronaut

A U.S. president

an RV

a bus

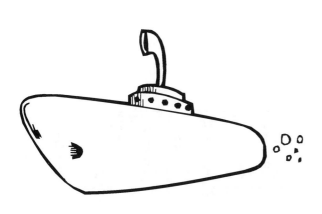

a submarine

a tent

115

a log cabin

a grass hut

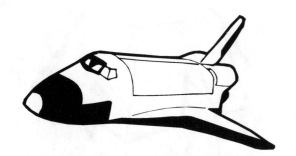

a space shuttle

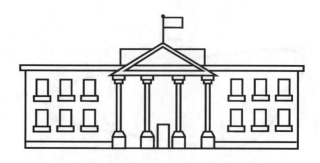

the White House

Carly Bear, What Will You Wear?

Model Story: *Jesse Bear, What Will You Wear?* (1996)
by Nancy White Carlstrom
New York: Little Simon

Description: Rhythm, rhyming text, and illustrations combine to describe Jesse Bear's activities and clothing changes from morning to bedtime in this 26-page story.

Predictable Pattern: Carly Bear, what will you wear? What will you wear in the _____? I will wear _____.
          (season)   (clothing)

Notes: There are two options for creating this pattern book: (1) one season could be depicted or (2) all the seasons could be represented on alternating pages (e.g., winter on the first page, spring on the second page, and so on). Have children complete the predictable pattern with a season and an appropriate item of clothing for that season. On the final page (the bottom half of page 120), children can draw what they look like in one of the seasons.

Goals: 1. *Phonology*
          Reduce gliding
          Reduce fronting
          Reduce vocalization
          Reduce assimilation
          Produce semivowel /r/
          Produce /l/
          Produce /k/

2. *Syntax*

Comprehend and use question forms (what)

Comprehend and use verb forms (future)

Comprehend and use morphological forms
(plurals, articles)

Comprehend and use pronouns

3. *Semantics*

Comprehend and use time concepts (seasons)

Comprehend and use quality concepts (descriptors)

4. *Thinking Skills*

Make associations

Establish causality

Categorize objects

Themes: Time (seasons)

Clothing

Additional Activities:

1. Read additional books:

Froggy Gets Dressed (1997)

by Jonathan London

New York: Viking

Description: Froggy wakes up and wants to play in the snow. Each time he goes outside, he realizes he forgot to put on another piece of clothing. By the time he has everything he needs, he is too tired to play, so he goes back to bed.

The Jacket I Wear in the Snow (1989)

by Shirley Neitzel

New York: Greenwillow Books

Description: A young girl names all the clothes that she must wear to play in the snow. This story uses rhymes and rebus pictures.

118

2. Write the following sentences on strips to fit in a pocket chart. Fill in the sentences with words or pictures of activities associated with each particular time of day.

   In the morning, I _____.
   In the afternoon, I _____.
   In the evening, I _____.

3. Cut out pictures of clothing from magazines and/or catalogs. Categorize the items based on the four seasons. Then make a collage for each season. Label the collages with season names. Have children take turns asking each other the predictable pattern question. Whenever children are asked the question, they should reply with the name of a clothing item from the corresponding collage or give their own appropriate responses.

4. Use a pattern of a bear or a child and dress it by coloring or gluing on appropriate clothing for a particular season. Then children can tell an activity they might do while wearing the seasonal clothes.

5. While reading the model story, emphasize the first word of each rhyming pair. Then have the children supply a word that rhymes with the word provided.

Carly Bear, What Will You Wear?

by _____

This is what I look like in the _____.

(season)

120

Carly Bear, what will you wear?
What will you wear in the _____?
(season)

I will wear
_____.
(clothing)

Carly Bear, what will you wear?
What will you wear in the _____?
(season)

I will wear
_____.
(clothing)

© 2000 Thinking Publications

Carly Bear, what will you wear?
What will you wear in the _____?

(season)

I will wear

_____.

(clothing)

Carly Bear, what will you wear?
What will you wear in the _____?

(season)

I will wear

_____.

(clothing)

122

boots

long pants

shorts

a long-sleeve shirt

© 2000 Thinking Publications

a short-sleeve shirt

a snowsuit

a jacket

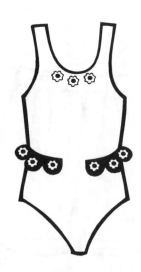

a swimsuit

mittens

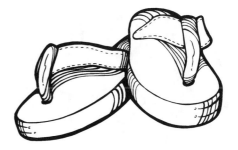

sandals

socks

a hat

© 2000 Thinking Publications

a sweater

gym shoes

a jogging suit

a scarf

Come and Play, Friend!
Come and Play, Creature!
Come and Play, Animal Friend!

Model Story: *Go Away, Big Green Monster!* (1993)
by Ed Emberly
Boston: Little, Brown

Description: In this 10-page book, a monster is slowly revealed through die-cut pages. Then the monster is gradually warned to go away and piece by piece its parts disappear.

Predictable Patterns:

Friend: "Come and play," I say to my friend with _____,
(descriptor)

_____ _____.
(descriptor)   (body part)

Creature: "Come and play," I say to the creature with _____,
(descriptor)

_____ _____.
(descriptor)   (body part)

Animal Friend: "Come and play," I say to my animal friend with

_____ _____.
(descriptor)   (body part)

Notes: There are three different pattern books that go along with this model story. For each story, have children complete the predictable pattern with descriptors and the corresponding body part. For *Come and Play, Friend!* the title page and final page are on page 130 and the pattern pages are on page 131. Children can draw a complete picture of a friend on the final page. Children can draw their own illustrations to go along with this pattern story. For a more difficult task, read the following directions to children, having them complete one pattern page for each facial part and then draw a composite picture of a friend on the final page. Descriptors of a friend could include:

(page 1) a big, circular face
(page 2) two, tiny ears
(page 3) big, brown eyes
(page 4) purple, triangular glasses
(page 5) a small, oval nose
(page 6) tiny, red freckles
(page 7) crooked, white teeth
(page 8) blond, curly hair

For *Come and Play, Creature!* the title page and final page are on page 132, the pattern pages are on page 133, and the illustrations are on pages 134–135. On the final page, children can draw a composite picture of their wooly mammoth-like creatures.

For *Come and Play, Animal Friend!* the title page and final page are on page 136, the pattern pages are on page 137, and the illustrations are on pages 138–139. (Older students can draw an animal as long as it meets descriptive criteria.) On the final page, children can draw a picture of their favorite animal.

Goals: 1. *Phonology*
Reduce final consonant deletion (FCD)
Reduce deaffrication
Reduce fronting
Reduce cluster simplification (CS)
Produce /k/
Produce /r/
Produce /l/
Produce /θ/
Produce /m/
Produce /tʃ/

2. *Syntax*
Comprehend and use verb forms (present)
Comprehend and use sentence structures (complex)

Comprehend and use morphological forms
(possessives, articles)
Comprehend and use pronouns

3. *Semantics*
Comprehend and use quality concepts (descriptors)
Comprehend and use quantity concepts (numbers)

4. *Thinking Skills*
Make associations
Draw inferences
Identify absurdities

Themes: Imagination
Body parts
Animals
People (friendship)

Additional Activities:

1. Read an additional book:
   Spotted Yellow Frogs: Fold-Out Fun with Patterns, Colors, 3-D Shapes, and Animals
   (1998)
   by Matthew Van Fleet
   New York: Dial Books

   Description: Animals are hiding behind fold-out geometric shapes.

2. Play a barrier game to develop following directions skills. Provide children with paper, drawing and coloring utensils, and a book or folder to use as a barrier. Have children work in pairs, taking turns giving each other directions and attempting to create identical illustrations of friends and/or unusual creatures.

3. Make a list of facial characteristics of children in the class. Graph the dominant attributes (e.g., hair color, eye color, teeth missing, dimples, hair length).

Come and Play, Friend!

by _____

Come and play! I want a friend. I like you.

130

"Come and play,"

I say to my friend with

_____,

(descriptor)

_____

(descriptor)

_____.

(body part)

"Come and play,"

I say to my friend with

_____,

(descriptor)

_____

(descriptor)

_____.

(body part)

131

© 2000 Thinking Publications

Come and Play, Creature!

by _____

Come and play! I want a friend. I like you.

"Come and play,"

I say to the creature with

_____,

(descriptor)

_____

(descriptor)

_____.

(body part)

"Come and play,"

I say to the creature with

_____,

(descriptor)

_____

(descriptor)

_____.

(body part)

three, little eyes

a long, squiggly trunk

huge, floppy ears

a fat, hairy body

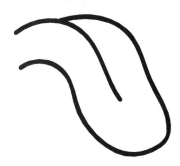

a wide, pink tongue

four, round paws

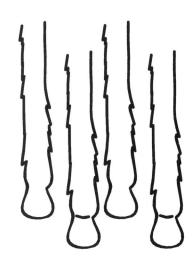

long, furry legs

a tiny, thin tail

Come and Play, Animal Friend!

by _____

Come and play! I want a friend. I like you.

"Come and play,"

I say to my animal

friend with

_____

(descriptor)

_____.

(body part)

"Come and play,"

I say to my animal

friend with

_____

(descriptor)

_____.

(body part)

137   © 2000 Thinking Publications

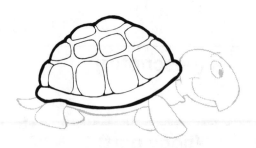

a hard shell

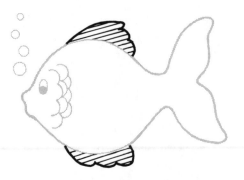

a wet fin

big feathers

colorful wings

138

a long tail

floppy ears

spindly legs

a striped back

© 2000 Thinking Publications

STORY PROFILES

A Dark, Dark Cave
A Hot, Hot Desert

Model Story: *A Dark, Dark Tale* (1992)
by Ruth Brown
New York: E.P. Dutton

Description: This is a 32-page story of a journey beginning on a dark, dark moor and progressing through the woods. The story continues until it reaches a house where there is a mouse in a dark, dark box.

Predictable Patterns:

A Dark, Dark Cave: In a dark, dark cave, there is a dark, dark _____.
(animal or object)

A Hot, Hot Desert: In the hot, hot desert, there is a hot, hot _____.
(animal or object)

Notes: Two different pattern books are provided as options. Complete either predictable pattern with an animal or object.

For *A Dark, Dark Cave,* the title page and final page are on page 143. The pattern pages are on page 144, and the illustrations are on pages 145–146. Have children draw a view of an opening in the cave on the final page of this story.

For *A Hot, Hot Desert,* the title page and final page are on page 147. The pattern pages are on page 148, and the illustrations are on pages 149–150. Have children draw a desert scene on the final page of this story.

Goals: 1. *Phonology*

Reduce vocalization

Reduce assimilation

Reduce fronting

Reduce final consonant deletion (FCD)

Produce /v/

Produce semivowel /r/

Produce /k/

Produce /t/

Produce /ð/

2. *Syntax*

Comprehend and use verb forms (copula)

Comprehend and use sentence structures (complex)

Comprehend and use morphological forms (articles)

3. *Semantics*

Comprehend and use spatial concepts (in)

Comprehend and use quality concepts (descriptors)

4. *Thinking Skills*

Make associations

Categorize objects

Themes: Places

Nature

Additional Activities: 1. Read an additional book:

We're Going on a Bear Hunt (1989)

by Michael Rosen

New York: Margaret McElderry

Description: This story tells of the exciting adventure of a family that treks over hill and dale to find a bear and then narrowly escapes danger when they find one!

2. Brainstorm with students to name real and nonsense rhyming words for *hot* and *dark*. List these words where everyone can see them.

3. Have children name forest animals and desert animals. Help them categorize each animal based on where it lives (forest or desert).

4. Discuss the following terrains: mountains, deserts, hills, and valleys. Have children locate pictures of the various terrains and use the pictures to assemble a map, or help them make a model of the various terrains out of clay or sand. Using pawns or toy figurines, have children navigate around the map or model while following your directions or while giving and following directions with each other (e.g., "Walk around the mountain," "Go over the hill," "Walk through the valley").

5. Have the children tell the route they take as they walk or ride to school, identifying landmarks, and using spatial descriptions (e.g., over the railroad tracks, under a bridge). Have them make a map of the route and explain it to the whole class or group.

A Dark, Dark Cave

by _____

Look, an opening to crawl out!

In a dark, dark
cave, there is a
dark, dark

_____.

(animal or object)

In a dark, dark
cave, there is a
dark, dark

_____.

(animal or object)

bat

bear

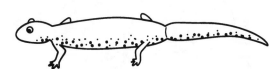

salamander

pool of water

145

rock

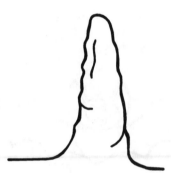

stalagmite

spider

treasure

146

A Hot, Hot Desert

by _____

A cool breeze at night!

In a hot, hot desert, there is a hot, hot

_____.

(animal or object)

In a hot, hot desert, there is a hot, hot

_____.

(animal or object)

148

cactus

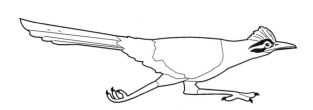

roadrunner

sand pile

camel

© 2000 Thinking Publications

lizard

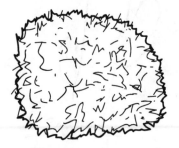

tumbleweed

snake

sand dune

150

 **STORY PROFILE**

Each Pickle Pumpkin Pie

Model Story: ***Each Peach Pear Plum*** (1999)
by Janet and Allan Ahlberg
New York: Penguin

Description: In this 32-page book, the reader plays with your eye as you play I Spy, finding nursery rhyme and fairy tale characters.

Predictable Pattern: Each pickle pumpkin pie.
Can you say the rhyme _____?
(nursery rhyme)

Notes: Complete the predictable pattern with a different nursery rhyme and then say the rhyme. The final page is on the bottom half of page 154. On that page, children can choose their favorite nursery rhyme, illustrate it, and then tell it.

Goals: 1. *Phonology*
Reduce gliding
Reduce fronting
Reduce deaffrication
Reduce vocalization
Reduce cluster simplification (CS)
Produce /ʧ/
Produce /r/ and semivowel /r/
Produce /p/
Produce /k/
Produce /l/

2. *Syntax*
Comprehend and use question forms (yes/no)

Comprehend and use verb forms
    (present, modal)
Comprehend and use morphological forms
    (articles, possessives)
Comprehend and use pronouns

3. *Semantics*
Comprehend and use spatial concepts
    (up, down, in, on)
Comprehend and use quality concepts (descriptors)

4. *Thinking Skill*
Sequence events or objects

Theme: Rhymes (nursery)

Additional Activities:

1. Read an additional book:
   Peek-a-Boo! (1997)
   by Janet and Allan Ahlberg
   New York: Viking

   Description: Brief rhyming clues invite children to look through actual holes cut in the pages, through which they see sunny, unsentimental views of the baby's world from breakfast to bedtime.

2. Create an interactive language chart using the sentences in the framed boxes below and on the following page. Refer to the procedures provided in Appendix H (page 379) for creating and using an interactive language chart.

Hickory, dickory, dock.

The mouse went up the clock.

The clock struck _____,

The mouse went down.

Hickory, dickory, dock.

> Humpty Dumpty sat on a _____.
>
> Humpty Dumpty had a great fall.
>
> All the king's horses
>
> And all the king's men
>
> Couldn't put Humpty together again.

3. Play the game I Spy using objects from the environment (e.g., "I spy something that crawls and it rhymes with rug" [bug], "I spy something on my feet and it rhymes with two" [shoe]).

4. Recite other songs, fingerplays, and/or nursery rhymes that contain gestures. Some possible options include:

   - If You're Happy and You Know It
   - I'm a Little Teapot
   - Teddy Bear, Teddy Bear, Turn Around

Each Pickle Pumpkin Pie

by _____

My favorite rhyme is _____**.**

I can say it for you!

Each pickle pumpkin pie.

Can you say the rhyme _____**?**
(nursery rhyme)

Each pickle pumpkin pie.

Can you say the rhyme _____**?**
(nursery rhyme)

Jack and Jill

Pat-a-Cake

Old Mother Hubbard

Little Bo-Peep

Hickory, Dickory, Dock

Twinkle, Twinkle, Little Star

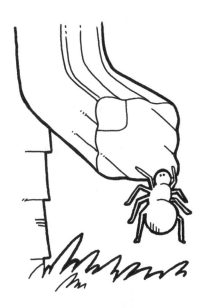

Itsy, Bitsy Spider

Humpty Dumpty

STORY PROFILE

Five Little Monkeys

Model Story: ***Five Little Monkeys Sitting in a Tree*** (1999)
by Eileen Christelow
New York: Houghton Mifflin

Description: In this 28-page book, Mama takes a nap while her five little monkeys tease Mr. Crocodile. "Can't catch me!" they shout, and Mr. Crocodile opens his big mouth. Snap! Now there are only four little monkeys, or so it seems.

Predictable Pattern: ____ little monkeys are _____ at the
(number)   (activity)

playground and having so much fun!

Notes: Children should complete the predictable pattern with a number and an activity. The number on the predictable pattern is left blank so that more than five monkeys can be used, if desired. (Draw in additional monkeys on the illustrations and change the number on the title page when using more than five monkeys.) The final page is on the bottom half of page 161. On the final page, children can draw their favorite playground activity.

Goals: 1. *Phonology*
Reduce gliding
Reduce fronting
Reduce stopping
Reduce cluster simplification (CS)
Reduce final consonant deletion (FCD)

Reduce vocalization

Reduce assimilation

Produce /l/

Produce /k/ and /g/

Produce /p/ and /m/

Produce /f/

Produce /s/

Produce /tʃ/

Produce semivowel /r/

2. *Syntax*

Comprehend and use verb forms
(present progressive)

Comprehend and use sentence structures
(compound)

Comprehend and use morphological forms
(plurals, possessives, articles)

3. *Semantics*

Comprehend and use quantity concepts (numbers)

Comprehend and use spatial concepts
(in, on, over, down)

4. *Thinking Skills*

Make associations

Categorize objects

Themes: Counting

Actions

School

Additional Activities: 1. Read an additional book:

Five Little Monkeys Jumping on the Bed (1998)

by Eileen Christelow

New York: Houghton Mifflin

Description: Five little monkeys ready themselves
for bed and say good night to their
mother. Then they really get down to

business as they launch into some serious bed jumping.

2. Have children draw a map of a playground they are familiar with, and help them label the different pieces of equipment. Then have them talk about about what they do on each piece of equipment (e.g., "I swing from the monkey bars").

3. Talk about a monkey's favorite food—bananas. Make banana splits, banana milkshakes, peanut butter and banana sandwiches, or banana bread following the directions in a recipe.

4. Perform the "Five Little Monkeys" fingerplay with the following actions:

Five little monkeys jumping on the bed.
(hold one hand on top of the other hand and bounce hand up and down)

One fell off and bumped his head.
(hold your index finger up and pretend to fall off the bed)

Mama called the doctor and the doctor said,
(hold your hand up to your ear)

"No more monkeys jumping on the bed."
(shake index finger)

(repeat with "Four little monkeys...," holding up four fingers; "Three little monkeys...," holding up three fingers; "Two little monkeys...," holding up two fingers; and "One little monkey...," holding up one finger)

No more monkeys jumping on the bed!
(shake index finger)

Five Little Monkeys

by _____

My favorite activity on the playground

is _____.

(activity)

_____

(number)

little monkeys are

_____

(activity)

**at the playground and
having so much fun!**

_____

(number)

little monkeys are

_____

(activity)

**at the playground and
having so much fun!**

swinging on swings

**digging in
the sandbox**

climbing on bars

sliding down poles

163

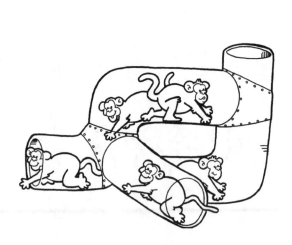

crawling through tunnels

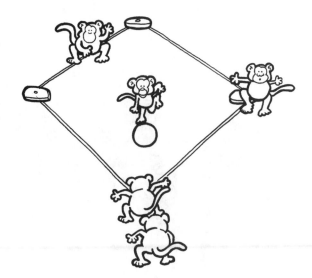

playing with a kickball

bouncing basketballs

jumping over a rope

STORY PROFILE

For Sale

Model Story: ***Caps for Sale*** (1999)
by Esphyr Slobodkina
New York: HarperCollins

Description: A peddler trying to sell caps takes a rest and sleeps under a tree while monkeys take all his caps up into a tree. He tries various methods to get his caps back from the monkeys. This is a 48-page book.

Predictable Pattern: _____ for sale. Fifty cents a _____.
            (object)   (object)

I want a _____ _____.
             (descriptor)   (object)

Notes: Have children complete the first two blanks and the last blank of the predictable pattern with the same object name (e.g., *cup, block)*. The third blank of the predictable pattern should contain a color or size descriptor, depending on what each particular illustration requires. Have children choose the color(s) for the objects that require a particular color and then color them. The final page is on the bottom half of page 168. Children can add up the amount of money they would spend if they bought all the items in their book, and put this number on the final page.

Goals: 1. *Phonology*
Reduce stopping
Reduce fronting
Produce /f/
Produce /s/
Produce /k/

2. *Syntax*

Comprehend and use verb forms
 (present, irregular past)

Comprehend and use morphological forms (articles)

Comprehend and use pronouns

3. *Semantics*

Comprehend and use quality concepts
 (colors, size)

4. *Thinking Skill*

Make comparisons

Themes: Colors

Counting

Additional Activities:

1. Read an additional book:

Mouse Paint (1999)

by Ellen Stoll Walsh

Topeka, KS: Econo-Clad Books

Description: Three white mice discover jars of red, blue, and yellow paint and explore the world of color.

2. Create an interactive language chart using the sentences in the framed box below. Refer to the procedures provided in Appendix H (page 379) for creating and using an interactive language chart.

Monkeys, monkeys in the tree.

Throw the _____ cap down to me.
                (color)

Put it _____.
        (prepositional phrase)

Place a peddler, a tree, and monkeys on the chart. State the prepositional phrase in relation to peddler (e.g., *under the peddler, next to the peddler, in front of the peddler, in back of the peddler, above the peddler*).

3. Have children identify the names of coins and their worth. Talk about the many ways to make 50 cents with the different coins.

4. Students can tell or write simple math story problems by figuring out how much change there would be from a dollar if one cap was purchased. Then talk about how much two caps, three caps, and four caps would cost. Help students count by 5s and by 10s.

5. Have children try to balance multiple caps on their heads. Problem-solve how the peddler kept the caps on his head and how he might get a cap down.

6. Play Simon Says using copies of the pictures of all the /k/ words on pages 170–173. Sample directions might include:

   "Simon says, point to the vehicle that starts with the /k/ sound."

   "Simon says, hold up something sweet and small that begins with /k/."

For Sale

by _____

How much did I spend?

I spent _____.
(amount)

_____ **for sale. Fifty cents a** _____.
(object)   **(object)**

I want a _____ _____.
                    (descriptor)   **(object)**

_____ **for sale. Fifty cents a** _____.
(object)   **(object)**

I want a _____ _____.
                    (descriptor)   **(object)**

169   © 2000 Thinking Publications

_____ **candy**
(color)

_____ **candy**
(color)

small cookie

medium cookie

large cookie

_____ **kite**
(color)

_____ **kite**
(color)

small cup

medium cup

large cup

　171

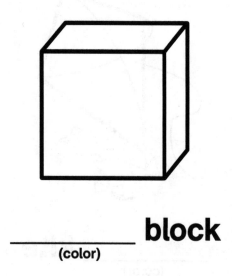

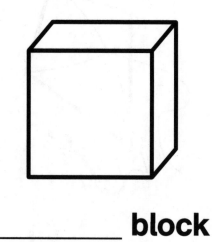

_____ **block**
(color)

_____ **block**

small card

medium card

large card

_____ **book**
(color)

_____ **book**
(color)

small car

medium car

large car

STORY PROFILE

From Here to There

Model Story: *From Head to Toe* (1999)
by Eric Carle
New York: HarperTrophy

Description: In this 32-page book, a host of pictured animals invite a child to imitate their actions, using a question-and-answer format.

Predictable Pattern: I am _____, and I can _____.
(athlete) (action)

Can you do it? I can do it!

Notes: Children should complete the predictable pattern with an athlete and an action (e.g., ice skater—jump in the air, baseball player—hit the ball). Complete the first space on the final page (bottom half of page 177) with a child's name. Complete the second space with an activity the child likes to do. Then draw the associated action.

Goals: 1. *Phonology*
Reduce fronting
Reduce final consonant deletion (FCD)
Reduce vocalization
Reduce weak syllable deletion (WSD)
Reduce stopping
Produce /k/
Produce semivowel /r/
Produce /l/
Produce /t/
Produce /ð/

2. *Syntax*

Comprehend and use verb forms
  (copula, modal)

Comprehend and use question forms (yes/no)

Comprehend and use sentence structures
  (compound)

Comprehend and use morphological forms
  (articles, noun + *er)*

Comprehend and use pronouns

3. *Thinking Skill*

Making associations

Themes: People (sports)

Actions

Additional Activities:

1. Read additional books:

This Is the Way We Make a Face (1996)

by Jo Lodge

New York: Barron's Juveniles

Description: A favorite nursery rhyme song is joined with the action of pull tabs so that each animal friend makes a funny face.

If You Hopped Like a Frog (1999)

by David M. Schwartz

New York: Scholastic

Description: Did you know that a frog can jump 20 times its body weight? Or that an ant can lift an object 50 times its weight? By applying these ratios and proportions to their own bodies, readers discover what they could do if they had the amazing abilities of animals.

2. Have students take turns being Simon while playing Simon Says. Simon can describe an action, or a

sequence of actions, that a particular athlete performs (e.g., "Simon says put on your helmet, get on your bike, and ride real fast," "Simon says tie your tennis shoes, dribble the basketball, and shoot a basket"). The other students must repeat the action or sequence whenever they hear the key phrase "Simon says."

3. Play Telephone using statements from the pattern book (e.g., "I am a swimmer and I can hold my breath in the water," "I am a basketball player and I can dribble a basketball"). Let students know that picturing the action in their minds can help them recall the athlete and the entire sentence.

4. Locate illustrations or photographs of a variety of animals (use the pictures on pages 345–346 and 349–350, if desired). Have children sit or stand in a circle. Have students take turns selecting an animal picture, standing in the middle of the circle, and pantomiming several of the animals actions while the rest of the students guess the animal.

From Here To There

by _____

I am

_____,
(name)

and I can move like all of these active people.

Can you

_____?
(action)

I am

_____,

(athlete)

and I can

_____.

(action)

Can you do it?
I can do it!

I am

_____,

(athlete)

and I can

_____.

(action)

Can you do it?
I can do it!

178

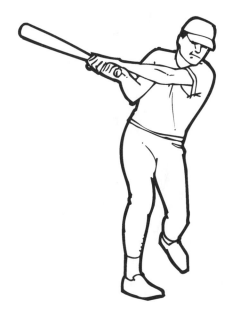

a baseball player

a weightlifter

a basketball player

a soccer player

179

a swimmer

an aerobics instructor

a gymnast

an ice skater

180

STORY PROFILES

Hannah, Hannah, What Do You Hear?
Amanda, Amanda, What Did You Taste?

Model Story: *Polar Bear, Polar Bear, What Do You Hear?* (1997)
by Bill Martin, Jr.
New York: Holt

Description: This is a colorful, 26-page book. Zoo animals, ranging from a polar bear to a walrus, make their distinctive sounds for each other while children imitate the sounds for the zookeeper.

Predictable Patterns:

Hannah: Hannah, Hannah, what do you hear? I hear a

_____: _____.
      (object)   (sound)

Amanda: Amanda, Amanda, what did you taste? I tasted

_____ _____.
   (descriptor)   (object)

Notes: Two different pattern books are provided. For *Hannah, Hannah, What Do You Hear?* have children complete the predictable pattern with an object and its corresponding sound. The sounds can be imitated orally or played from a prerecorded audiotape. The title page and final page are on page 184, the pattern pages are on page 185, and the illustrations are on pages 186–187. Children can draw a picture of the object that makes their favorite sound on the final page.

For *Amanda, Amanda, What Did You Taste?* children should complete the predictable patterns with a description of an object and the corresponding object.

The final page is on the bottom half of page 188. Children can draw a picture of their favorite food on that page. The pattern pages are on page 189. Consider having children taste the actual food items as they select illustrations from pages 190–191 for their books.

Goals: 1. *Phonology*
Reduce vocalization
Reduce cluster simplification (CS)
Produce semivowel /r/
Produce /t/
Produce /d/
Produce /s/

2. *Syntax*
Comprehend and use verb forms
    (present, modal, past, infinitive)
Comprehend and use question forms (what)
Comprehend and use morphological forms
    (plurals, articles)
Comprehend and use pronouns

3. *Semantics*
Comprehend and use quality concepts (descriptors)

4. *Thinking Skills*
Make associations
Predict events

Themes: Body parts
Food
Actions

Additional Activities: 1. Read additional books:
Brown Bear, Brown Bear, What Do You See?
(1983)
by Bill Martin, Jr., illustrated by Eric Carle
New York: Holt, Rinehart and Winston

Description: Familiar animals, ranging from a bear to a fish, see each other and then see a teacher and children.

Pat the Bunny (1999)

by Dorothy Kunhardt

New York: Golden Books

Description: Play along with Paul and Judy as they smell the flowers, look in the mirror, play peek-a-boo, and, of course, pat the bunny.

2. Create an interactive language chart using the sentences in the framed boxes below. Refer to the procedures provided in Appendix H (page 379) for creating and using an interactive language chart.

> Hannah, Hannah, what do you hear?
>
> I hear a _____: _____.
>   (object)   (sound)

> Amanda, Amanda, what did you taste?
>
> I tasted a _____ _____.
>   (descriptor)   (object)

(Children's names could be substituted for Hannah or Amanda.)

3. Have children taste a variety of foods. Talk about if the foods taste bitter, sour, sweet, or salty. Then children can be blindfolded and given foods to taste as they guess what each item might be.

4. Post pictures of musical instruments around the room. Have students listen to recordings of musical instruments and attempt to identify each sound.

5. Play a commercially available Sound Bingo game.

6. Talk about the five senses. Then categorize objects and/or pictures based on which of the senses would be stimulated by each item.

Hannah, Hannah, What Do You Hear?

by _____

My favorite thing to listen to is _____.

(object)

Hannah, Hannah, what do you hear?

I hear a _____: _____.

             (object)   **(sound)**

Hannah, Hannah, what do you hear?

I hear a _____: _____.

             (object)   **(sound)**

telephone

ring, ring

car

beep, beep

baby

waa, waa

person

ha, ha

balloon

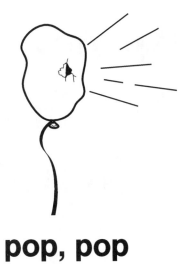

pop, pop

train

choo, choo

doorbell

ding, dong

clock

tick, tock

Amanda, Amanda, What Did You Taste?

by _____

My favorite thing to eat is _____.

(food)

Amanda, Amanda, what did you taste?

I tasted _____ _____.
                      (descriptor)   **(object)**

Amanda, Amanda, what did you taste?

I tasted _____ _____.
                      (descriptor)   **(object)**

salty pretzels

salty peanuts

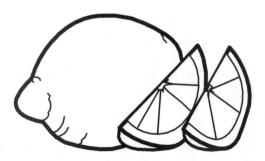

sour lemons

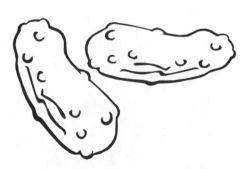

sour pickles

190

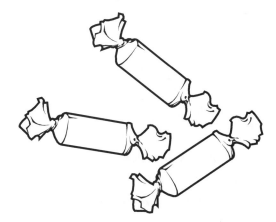

sweet candy

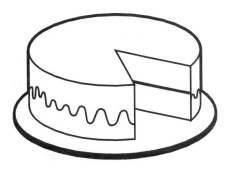

sweet cake

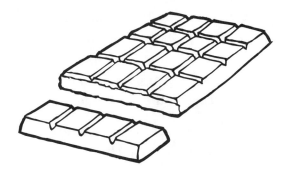

bitter chocolate

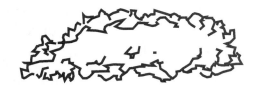

bitter parsley

Hi, Pizza Boy! (Animals)
Hi, Pizza Boy! (Seasonal Characters)

Model Story: *"Hi, Pizza Man!"* (1998)
by Virginia Walter
New York: Orchard Books

Description: Getting hungrier and hungrier while waiting for a pizza to be delivered, Vivian imagines possible disguises for the pizza man. This is a 32-page book.

Predictable Patterns:

Animals: What if it's a pizza _____. Then what will you
(animal)

say? _____, _____, pizza _____!
(animal sound) (animal sound)   (animal)

Seasonal Characters: What if it's a pizza _____. Then what will you
(character)

say? Hi pizza _____! It's the month of _____!
(character)   (month)

Notes: There are two variations for this model story: animals and seasonal characters. For the animals book, children should complete the predictable pattern with animal names and noises. The title page and final page are on page 195, the pattern pages are on page 196, and the illustrations are on pages 197–198. Children can draw a picture of a real or imaginary animal or person delivering pizza on the final page.

For the seasonal characters book, children should complete the predictable pattern with a character and month. (See Additional Activity #6 for the pairings of the months and characters.) The title page

and final page are on page 199, the pattern pages
are on page 200, and the illustrations are on pages
201–203. Children can draw a picture of a real or
imaginary person delivering pizza on the final page.

Goals: 1. *Phonology*
Reduce final consonant deletion (FCD)
Reduce stopping
Produce /p/
Produce /t/
Produce /s/
Produce /f/
Produce /b/

2. *Syntax*
Comprehend and use negation
Comprehend and use question forms (what)
Comprehend and sentence structures (complex)
Comprehend and use morphological forms (articles)
Comprehend and use verb forms
(copula, modal, future)

3. *Semantics*
Comprehend and use quality concepts (descriptors)

4. *Thinking Skills*
Predict events
Draw inferences
Make associations

Themes: People
Animals
Time (months)
Clothing

**Additional
Activities:** 1. Read an additional book:
The Doorbell Rang (1994)
by Pat Hutchins
New York: Mulberry Books

Description: A large plate of cookies gets smaller
and smaller as more visitors arrive.

2. Draw a circular pizza on a sheet of poster board. Cut the pizza into eight equal pieces. Have children count the pieces. Talk about how many pieces make a whole, a half, and a quarter of a pizza. The pizza could also be made into different shapes. As another option, use Play-Doh to make the pizzas.

3. Talk about safety issues regarding opening doors to strangers and answering phones. Role-play safe routines.

4. Have a pizza party! Follow a recipe to make a pizza. Let children be creative and design their own pizza with toppings of their choice. Categorize the pizza toppings into food groups or favorite items.

5. Problem-solve by having students role-play ordering various meals a°t a restaurant. Practice scenarios for breakfast, lunch, and dinner.

6. Associate each character with its assigned month when using the seasonal characters pattern book and illustrations. Discuss the role that each character has in relation to the month (e.g., a sunbather is associated with the month of August since it is usually hot enough to lay out in the sun in that month). Below is a list of the 12 months and their associated characters:

January—snow person
February—U.S. president
March—leprechaun
April—bunny
May—soldier
June—graduate
July—flag carrier
August—sunbather
September—teacher
October—pumpkin
November—Pilgrim
December—reindeer

Hi,
Pizza Boy!

by _____

What will you say when the doorbell rings?

Hi, pizza boy!

What if it's not a pizza boy? What if it's a pizza _____. Then what will you say?
(animal)

_____, _____, **pizza** _____!
(animal sound)   (animal sound)   (animal)

What if it's not a pizza boy? What if it's a pizza _____. Then what will you say?
(animal)

_____, _____, **pizza** _____!
(animal sound)   (animal sound)   (animal)

frog

pig

horse

cow

sheep

chicken

bird

rooster

198

Hi, Pizza Boy!

by _____

What will you say when the doorbell rings?

Hi, pizza boy!

What if it's not a pizza boy? What if it's a

pizza _____. Then what will you say?
(character)

Hi pizza _____! It's the month of _____!
(character)   (month)

What if it's not a pizza boy? What if it's a

pizza _____. Then what will you say?
(character)

Hi pizza _____! It's the month of _____!
(character)   (month)

200

January

snow person

February

U.S. president

March

leprechaun

April

bunny

May

soldier

June

graduate

July

flag carrier

August

sunbather

September

teacher

October

pumpkin

November

Pilgrim

December

reindeer

STORY PROFILES

I Am Me! (People)
I Am Me! (Transportation)
I Am Me! (Dogs)

Model Story: *Quick As a Cricket* (1990)
by Audrey Wood
Swindon, UK: Child's Play

Description: Using animal similes, a young boy celebrates his self-awareness. Rhyming phrases are used throughout this 24-page book.

Predictable Pattern: I'm as _____ as _____.
  (descriptor)   (noun)

Notes: Children can complete this predictable pattern with a descriptor and a noun. Three different pattern books can be modeled after this story. *I Am Me! (People)* (illustrations are on pages 209–210) uses key features of a variety of jobs, relatives, or both. *I Am Me! (Transportation)* (illustrations are on pages 211–212) provides vehicle similes for children to consider. *I Am Me! (Dogs)* (illustrations are on pages 213–214) uses similes related to salient characteristics of familiar dogs. For all of the pattern books, the title page and final page are on page 207, and the pattern pages are on page 208. On the final pages, students can draw a picture of themselves and try to make their own simile.

Before students create their pattern books, talk about why each descriptor is appropriate for each noun (e.g., saying, "A tow truck is strong enough to pull a car, so we can call it powerful").

Goals: 1. *Phonology*
Reduce final consonant deletion (FCD)
Reduce stopping
Produce /z/
Produce /m/

2. *Syntax*
Comprehend and use verb forms (copula)
Comprehend and use pronouns
Comprehend and use morphological forms (articles)

3. *Semantics*
Comprehend and use quality concepts (descriptors)

4. *Thinking Skills*
Make associations
Make comparisons

Themes: People
Transportation
Animals (dogs)

Additional Activities: 1. Read an additional book:
When I Was Little: A Four-Year-Old's Memoir of Her Youth (1999)
by Jamie Lee Curtis
New York: HarperCollins

Description: A spirited tale about a 4-year-old who delights in all the things she can do now that she is no longer a baby.

2. Make a card deck of antonyms. Glue a variety of pictures and their corresponding text from pages 209–214 onto index cards. For each illustration used, write an opposite descriptive word and draw a picture corresponding to the opposite word on another card (e.g., *speedy racecar—slow snail; big airplane—little penny; short bassett hound—tall tree*). Students can match the opposites while playing a variety of

traditional card games (e.g., Go Fish, Memory, Old Maid).

3. Help children make personalized books to use as gifts for parents, grandparents, and other special relatives or friends. For example, if a child is creating a book for his or her mother, the inside pages could include phrases like "I am as friendly as my mom," "I am as funny as my dad," and "I am as curious as my brother." Use the child's drawings, photographs students bring from home, or pictures cut from magazines for the illustrations on each page.

4. After about one month of school, have children bring in a recent picture of themselves. Glue each picture onto a piece of poster board. Have classmates dictate or write positive qualities about each student on the poster board near his or her picture. Read each child's collage aloud to the class. Place the collages in the students' portfolios, or hang them up to be viewed during an open house or parent-teacher conference.

I Am Me!

by _____

And... I am ME!

I am as

_____
(descriptor)

as

_____ .
(noun)

I am as

_____
(descriptor)

as

_____ .
(noun)

energetic

a runner

helpful

a police officer

smart

a doctor

silly

a clown

caring

a parent

loving

a grandparent

friendly

a teacher

generous

a friend

speedy

a racecar

adventurous

a convertible

loud

a fire truck

big

an airplane

© 2000 Thinking Publications

bouncy

a monster truck

important

an ambulance

useful

a tug boat

powerful

a tow truck

skinny

a dachshund

short

a Basset Hound

tall

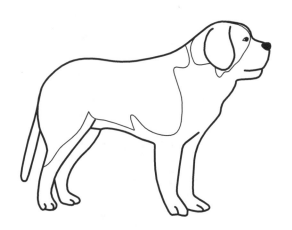

a St. Bernard

fast

a greyhound

spotted

a Dalmatian

protective

a rottweiller

gentle

a Labrador retriever

soft

an Irish setter

214

STORY PROFILES

I Like You, Animals
I Like You, Colors

Model Story: *I Love You, Mouse* (1990)
by John Graham
New York: Harcourt Brace

Description: A child imagines things he would do with various animals if he were one of them. This is a 32-page book.

Predictable Patterns:

Animals: I like you _____, and if I were a _____, I'd find
                (animal)   (animal)
you _____. Then we'd _____ together and
   (animal's home)   (action)
_____ _____.
  (action)   (noun)

Colors: I like you _____, and if I were _____, I'd be
             (color)   (color)
_____ and _____ _____.
  (object)   (action)   (noun)

Notes: Two different pattern books are provided. *For I Like You, Animals,* suggested words children could use to complete the predictable pattern are listed below:

fish—...a river, ...swim, ...eat worms
camel—...a desert, ...walk, ...eat plants
goat—a mountain, ...climb, ...graze on grass
porcupine—a forest, ...bristle, ...munch leaves
polar bear—an iceberg, ...float, ...catch fish
dolphin—an ocean, ...swim, ...eat fish
gorilla—a jungle, ...sit, ...eat bananas
snake—a forest, ...slither, ...eat mice

For this book, the title page and final page are on page 218, the pattern pages are on page 219, and the illustrations are on pages 220–221. Children could draw a circle (representing the world) filled in with a variety of animals on the final page.

For *I Like You, Colors,* suggested words children could use to complete the predictable pattern are listed below:

red—a traffic signal, ...stop cars
blue—a sky, ...carry clouds
yellow—a sunflower, ...feed birds
orange—a pumpkin, ...become a jack-o-lantern
purple—a flower, ...grow petals
green—a grasshopper, ...eat bugs
white—a cloud, ...give rain
black—night, ...twinkle stars

The title page and final page are on page 222, the pattern pages are on page 223, and the illustrations are on pages 224–225. Children could draw a circle (representing the world) filled in with a variety of colors on the final page.

Goals: 1. *Phonology*
    Reduce vocalization
    Reduce stopping
    Reduce fronting
    Reduce gliding
    Produce /r/ and semivowel /r/
    Produce /l/
    Produce /k/
    Produce /f/

2. *Syntax*
    Comprehend and use verb forms (modal, copula)
    Comprehend and use pronouns
    Comprehend and use sentence structures (complex)
    Comprehend and use morphological forms (articles)

3. *Semantics*
   Comprehend and use quality concepts (colors)

4. *Thinking Skills*
   Draw inferences
   Make associations

Themes: Animals
Places
Colors

Additional Activities:

1. Read an additional book:
   Mama, Do You Love Me? (1998)
   by Barbara M. Joosse
   New York: Chronicle Books

   Description: A small Inuit girl repeatedly asks her mother if she would love her even if she did mischievous things relating to the history of the Inuits.

2. Explore colors by having children bring in objects of an assigned color. Have children talk about their objects. Talk about light and dark shades of each color, and sort the objects accordingly.

3. When learning more about occupations, modify the *I Like You, Colors* pattern book to be an *I Like You, Workers* book. Change the title page and have students generate a list of occupations. Completed patterns might include "I like you, carpenter, and if I were a carpenter, I'd be a worker and build a house." Locate appropriate pictures or have children illustrate their books with original drawings. (Use the occupations pictures provided on pages 271–272, if desired.)

4. Look up pictures of animals and their habitats on the Internet or in library books. Talk about how the various animal homes are made.

I Like You, Animals

by _____

I like the whole world!

I like you _____, and if I were a
(animal)

_____, I'd find you _____. Then we'd
(animal)   (animal's home)

_____ together and _____ _____.
(action)   (action)   (noun)

I like you _____, and if I were a
(animal)

_____, I'd find you _____. Then we'd
(animal)   (animal's home)

_____ together and _____ _____.
(action)   (action)   (noun)

219

fish

camel

goat

porcupine

polar bear

dolphin

gorilla

snake

I Like You, Colors

by _____

I like the whole world!

222

I like you _____, and if I were _____,
(color)   (color)

I'd be _____ and _____ _____.
(object)   (action)   (noun)

I like you _____, and if I were _____,
(color)   (color)

I'd be _____ and _____ _____.
(object)   (action)   (noun)

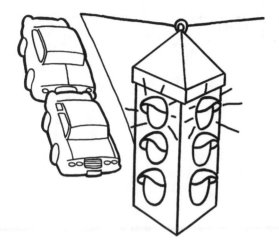

red

blue

yellow

orange

224

purple

green

white

black

© 2000 Thinking Publications

STORY PROFILES

I Think I Can, I Think I Can! (Sports)
I Think I Can, I Think I Can! (Chores)

Model Story: ***The Little Engine That Could*** (1990)
by Wally Piper
New York: Price Stern Sloan

Description: This 37-page book is a tale of motivation and positive thinking. A little engine overcomes the odds and pulls a train over a mountain.

Predictable Pattern: Right now, I cannot _____, but I
(hard activity)

think I can, I think I can _____.
(easy activity)

Notes: Two different pattern books are provided for this model story—one with a sports theme and one with a chores theme. For the sports book, children should complete the first blank of the predictable pattern with a task that would be too difficult and the second blank with an easier task. The title page and final page for the sports book are on page 229, the pattern pages are on page 230, and the illustrations are on pages 231–232. Children can draw a picture of themselves doing a sports activity on the final page and tell how it makes them feel.

For the chores book, children should complete the first blank of the predictable pattern with a chore that would be too difficult and the second blank with an easier chore. The title page and final page for the chores theme are on page 233, the pattern pages are on page 234, and the illustrations are on pages

235–236. On the final page, children can illustrate a chore that they think they can do and then tell how it makes them feel.

Goals:

1. *Phonology*
   Reduce stopping
   Reduce fronting
   Reduce assimilation
   Reduce final consonant deletion (FCD)
   Produce /θ/
   Produce /k/
   Produce /n/
   Produce /t/

2. *Syntax*
   Comprehend and use negation
   Comprehend and use verb forms (present, modal)
   Comprehend and use sentence structures (compound)
   Comprehend and use pronouns

3. *Thinking Skills*
   Draw inferences
   Make comparisons

Theme: Actions (sports, chores)

Additional Activities:

1. Read an additional book:
   Flap Your Wings and Try (1989)
   by Charlotte Pomerantz
   New York: Green Willow Books

   Description: Following the advice of family members, a young bird learns to fly. A lesson is learned: Many things are possible if you just try.

2. Discuss the idea of "personal best," relating how the little blue engine had a positive attitude about something he had never done before. Talk about his feeling of pride when he reached the other side of

the mountain. Use this idea to explain goal setting to children.

Have each child choose a short-term goal, and help him or her phrase the goal in terms of "I think I can, I think I can" (e.g., "I think I can, I think I can learn to count to 50"; "I think I can, I think I can learn to ride a bicycle"). Provide each child with a piece of paper cut in the shape of a train engine. Direct children to write their goal on their engine shapes and to draw a picture that represents the goal. Post the engines around the room where everyone can see them. When children achieve the goals, celebrate with them by noting their accomplishments through illustration or description in their "quality work" book kept for that school year (i.e., their portfolio).

3. Line up three boxes (e.g., shoe boxes or small appliance boxes) to represent the beginning, middle, and end of a train. Gather a variety of pictures of foods, animals, and toys or locate actual objects. Have students categorize items by sorting them into the three boxes. Children could be encouraged to think of additional categories by naming other items that a train might carry.

4. Children should understand that many skills need to be learned before they can be successful with certain tasks. Discuss how learning simple skills is important. Have children think of a difficult skill, and then help them list all the skills they need to learn to perform the more difficult skill. For example, before you can read a book, you must first learn the alphabet, learn to read simple words, and learn to read sentences.

I Think I Can, I Think I Can!

by _____

I think I can, I think I can _____,
(activity)

and it makes me feel _____!
(emotion)

© 2000 Thinking Publications

Right now, I cannot

_____,
(hard activity)

but I think I can,

I think I can

_____.
(easy activity)

Right now, I cannot

_____,
(hard activity)

but I think I can,

I think I can

_____.
(easy activity)

hit a home run

run the bases

jump a hurdle

jump over a rope

make a basket

bounce a ball

do a header

kick the ball

ski down a big hill

swim in deep water

play in the snow

blow bubbles

drive a racecar

win a horse race

play with a toy car

sit on a horse

I Think I Can,
I Think I Can!

by _____

I think I can, I think I can _____,
(activity)

and it makes me feel _____!
(emotion)

233

Right now, I cannot

_____,

(hard activity)

but I think I can,

I think I can

_____.

(easy activity)

Right now, I cannot

_____,

(hard activity)

but I think I can,

I think I can

_____.

(easy activity)

wash laundry

put clothes away

cook supper

set the table

vacuum

put toys away

make a shopping list

pick out a shirt

mow the grass

take out the trash

pick flowers

throw trash away

make my bed

drive a car

fluff my pillow

help wash the car

236

STORY PROFILE

Itchy, Itchy Mosquito Bites!

Model Story: *Itchy, Itchy Chicken Pox* (1992)
by Grace MacCarone
New York: Scholastic

Description: Peppy rhymes make this a lively story about the humorous side to a common ailment. This is a 32-page book.

Predictable Pattern: _____ spots on my _____.
(number)   (body part)

Itchy, itchy mosquito bites!

Notes: Children can complete the predictable pattern with the number of spots and the body part where the spots appear. The title page and final page are on page 240. Children can use the final page to draw a body part with 10 spots.

Goals: 1. *Phonology*
Reduce stopping
Reduce deaffrication
Reduce cluster simplification (CS)
Produce /ʧ/
Produce /s/
Produce /m/ and /b/

2. *Syntax*
Comprehend and use verb forms (present)
Comprehend and use morphological forms
(plurals, possessives)
Comprehend and use pronouns

3. *Semantics*

    Comprehend and use spatial concepts (on)

    Comprehend and use quantity concepts (numbers)

4. *Thinking Skills*

    Sequence events or objects

    Establish causality

Themes: Counting

Body parts

Additional Activities:

1. Read additional books:

    Piggies (1995)

    by Audrey Wood

    New York: Voyage

    Description: Ten little piggies dance on a young child's fingers and toes before finally going to sleep.

    The Lady with the Alligator Purse (1998)

    by Nadine Bernard Westcott

    New York: Little, Brown

    Description: Contains the old jump-rope rhyme featuring an ailing, young Tiny Tim.

2. Trace children's bodies onto large sheets of paper. Have children draw clothing and accessories on their traced bodies and then label their body parts.

3. Create a list of insects. Categorize the insects based on those that bite versus those that sting. Illustrations of insects can be found on pages 359–360.

4. Draw one silly monster with spots for each child, varying the number of spots on each monster. Help children guess whose monster has the most spots, the least spots, more spots than someone else's, and fewer spots than someone else's. Then

have children count the spots on their monsters. Make a graph plotting the number of spots on each child's monster.

5. Problem-solve what to do in the following situations:
   * Make a mosquito bite stop itching
   * Prevent mosquito bites
   * Make a bee sting stop hurting
   * Stay healthy after an illness

6. Discuss common childhood diseases, like chicken pox and measles, with children. Talk about what causes the diseases and how they are treated.

7. Talk about activities that happen during a routine visit to the doctor's office. Sequence the activities in a typical order.

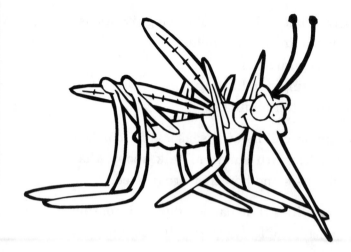

Itchy, Itchy Mosquito Bites!

by _____

---

10 spots on my _____.
(body part)

Itchy, itchy mosquito bites!

_____ **spots on my** _____.
(number)   (body part)

Itchy, itchy mosquito bites!

_____ **spots on my** _____.
(number)   (body part)

Itchy, itchy mosquito bites!

241

2

finger

3

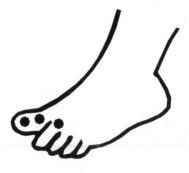

toes

4

cheek

5

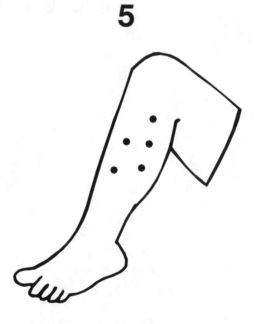

leg

6

arm

7

forehead

8

chin

9

stomach

STORY PROFILE

It's Not Safe!

Model Story: *No, David!* (1998)
by David Shannon
New York: Scholastic

Description: This 32-page book relates the author's personal experiences of hearing "No" from his mother during a day filled with mischievous behavior.

Predictable Pattern: Don't _____. It's not safe!
(activity)

Notes: Children should complete each predictable pattern page with a dangerous activity. The final page is on the bottom half of page 247. On the final page, children can draw a picture of a time when they made a safe choice instead of putting themselves in danger. Possible responses might include:

- Asking an adult to plug in an appliance
- Asking an adult to get a ball that rolled into the road
- Telling an adult when another child has matches
- Having an adult answer the door

Goals: 1. *Phonology*
Reduce cluster simplification (CS)
Reduce stopping
Reduce vocalization
Reduce gliding
Produce /s/
Produce /f/
Produce /r/ and semivowel /r/

Produce /l/

Produce /t/ and /d/

2. *Syntax*

Comprehend and use negation

Comprehend and use verb forms (copula)

Comprehend and use pronouns

3. *Thinking Skills*

Predict events

Establish causality

Theme: Actions (safety)

Additional Activities:

1. Read an additional book:

Even If I Did Something Awful (1992)

by Barbara Shook Hazen

New York: Aladdin

Description: Before revealing the awful thing she did, a child tries to get her mother's assurance of love.

2. Use the model book—*No, David!*—in conjunction with a school's safety week activities. Find out if the local fire department conducts special programs for schools. If not, invite a firefighter in to speak to the children about home safety.

3. Talk with students about things that might happen when they do not play with their toys appropriately or when they leave their toys in places that can cause accidents. Examples include leaving Rollerblades at the bottom of stairs, driving a small battery-powered car in the street, or riding in a wagon down the stairs.

4. Discuss with children why each "Don't" statement in their pattern book is unsafe. Ask children to think about safe alternatives to each situation

(e.g., waiting for an adult to get a ball that has rolled onto the street). Children can draw a picture of a safe alternative to each of the unsafe behaviors in their books. Have children take the drawings home to review periodically with their families.

5. Recommend safety-orientated books to parents. In addition to the model story and recommended additional story, consider the following list of books:

Mama, Do You Love Me? (1998)
by Barbara M. Joosse
New York: Chronicle Books

Alexander and the Terrible, Horrible, No Good, Very Bad Day (1987)
by Judith Viorst
New York: Aladdin

I Need a Hug! (1992)
by Bill Keane
New York: Fawcett Books

Guess How Much I Love You (1996)
by Sam McBratney
Cambridge, MA: Candlewick Press

6. Conduct a parent meeting devoted to thinking of ways to be positive toward children who are constantly being corrected at home.

7. Give parents a sign containing the the mnemonic "*IALAC*," which stands for **I A**m **L**ovable **A**nd **C**apable. Encourage parents to hang the sign in their home so that they are reminded to praise their children for the good they do instead of calling attention to negative behaviors only.

It's Not Safe!

by _____

I like to be safe!

Don't

_____

_____

_____ .

(activity)

It's not safe!

Don't

_____

_____

_____ .

(activity)

It's not safe!

**walk where there
is broken glass**

**hide inside when
your house is on fire**

play with matches

run onto the road

**grab a hot container
with your bare hands**

**plug in anything
when your hands
are wet**

**open the door
for strangers**

**play with cleaning
products**

STORY PROFILES

I've Been Working on My House
I've Been Working at My School

Model Story: *I've Been Working on the Railroad* (1996)
illustrated by Nadine Bernard Westcott
New York: Hyperion

Description: Arriving at the train station, a young boy is delighted when he is made an assistant conductor for the day. This is a 32-page book.

Predictable Patterns:

House: I've been working on my house with _____.
(object)

School: I've been working at my school on _____.
(activity)

Notes: Two different pattern books are provided. Children can complete the predictable pattern for *I've Been Working on My House* with the name of an object. The title page and final page are on page 254, the pattern pages are on page 255, and the illustrations are on pages 256–257. Children can draw a picture of their home on the final page.

Children can complete the predictable pattern for *I've Been Working at My School* with the name of an activity. The title page and final page are on page 258, the pattern pages are on page 259, and the illustrations are on pages 260–261. Children can draw a picture of their school on the final page.

Goals: 1. *Phonology*
Reduce fronting

Reduce final consonant deletion (FCD)

Reduce vocalization

Produce semivowel /r/

Produce /k/

Produce /s/

Produce /θ/

2. *Syntax*

Comprehend and use verb forms (past, participle)

Comprehend and use morphological forms
(possessives, articles, plurals)

Comprehend and use pronouns

3. *Thinking Skills*

Make associations

Categorize objects

Themes: Actions

School

Additional Activities:

1. Read an additional book:

This Is the House That Jack Built (1995)

illustrated by Pam Adams

Swindon, UK: Child's Play

Description: A cumulative nursery rhyme about the chain of events that started when Jack built a house. Includes die-cut pages.

2. To target more advanced language forms, change the predictable pattern to one of the following:

I could have been working on _____ but _____.

I should have been working on _____ but _____.

I would have been working on _____ but _____.

Write the new predictable patterns on strips of paper. Have children supply responses, and write the responses on short strips of paper. Use the sentence strips and response slips to make a variety of sentences.

3. Discuss the different people it takes to build a house or a school (e.g., carpenter, electrician, plumber, roofer, brick layer, drywaller, concrete pourer). Talk about each worker's job. Consider touring a building site or finding a "virtual tour" on the Internet.

4. Make a train using paper cut-outs. Create patterns for an engine and various train cars. Duplicate enough engines and train cars for each child to create his or her own train. Have children write their name on their engine. Then write a word on each train car related to a specific goal for the child. For example, each car could contain a different word from the child's phonology word list, a word from a science vocabulary list, or a math fact. Help children cut out their patterns. As children say or respond correctly to the item on each train car, have them attach the car to the engine with tape or glue.

I've Been Working on My House

by _____

I've been working on my house

all the live long day, to make it beautiful!

I've been working

on my house

with

_____.

(object)

I've been working

on my house

with

_____.

(object)

a paintbrush

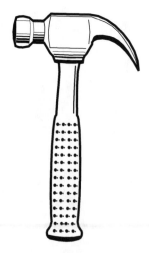

a hammer

a screwdriver

pliers

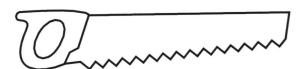

a saw

a wrench

a lawn mower

a ladder

257

I've Been Working at My School

by _____

I've been working at my school
all the live long day, doing my best!

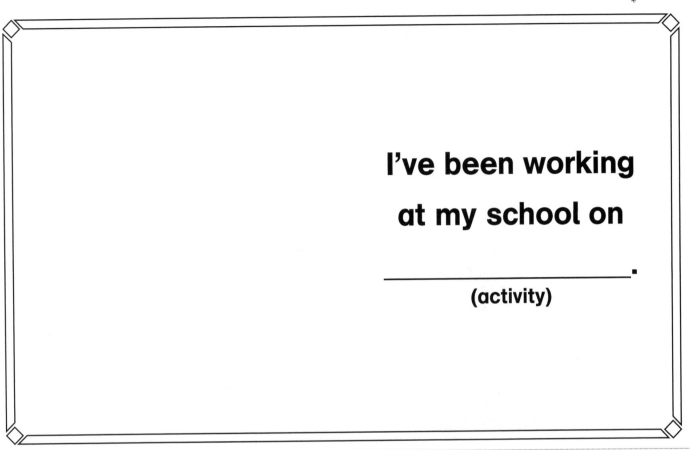

**I've been working
at my school on**

_____.

(activity)

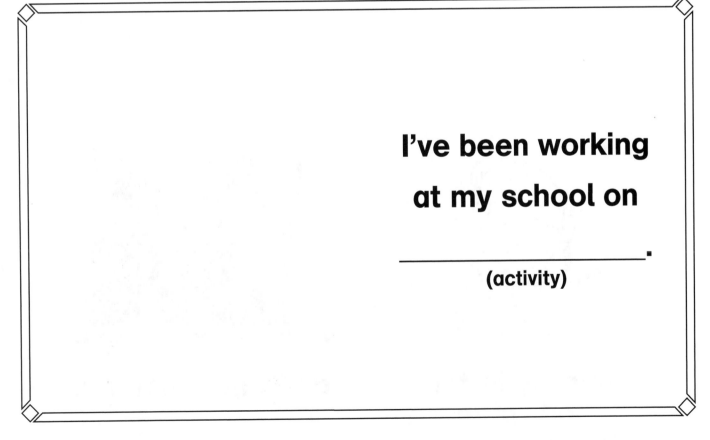

**I've been working
at my school on**

_____.

(activity)

© 2000 Thinking Publications

**drawing and
coloring**

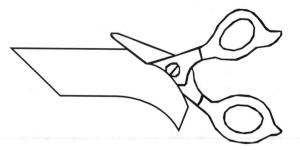

cutting

**making letters
and writing**

counting numbers

**listening and
following directions**

**cooperating with
my friends**

reading books

learning computers

© 2000 Thinking Publications

Jolly Joshua
Showy Shelly

Model Story: *Silly Sally* (1999)
by Audrey Wood
New York: Red Wagon Books

Description: In this 15-page book, Silly Sally goes to town by walking backwards and upside down. Along the way, she meets a variety of animals that complete the rhyming verses.

Predictable Patterns:

Joshua: Jolly Joshua went to _____, walking backwards,
(place)

upside down. On the way, he met _____.
(person)

Shelly: Showy Shelly went to _____, walking backwards,
(place)

upside down. On the way, she met _____.
(person)

Notes: Two variations of the same pattern book are provided, one with a boy character (Joshua) and one with a girl character (Shelly). Children can complete the first blank of either predictable pattern with the word *town* or the name of another specific place (such as McDonald's or the park) and the second blank with a person. For *Jolly Joshua,* the title page and final page are on page 265 and the pattern pages are on page 266. For *Showy Shelly,* the title page and final page are on page 267 and the pattern pages are on page 268. Children can be encouraged to think of their own locations and occupations, or they can choose from those illustrated on pages

269–272. When children choose to use both a location and an occupation illustration from those provided, the two pictures can be glued side by side on the pattern page. Children can draw a picture of themselves walking backwards and upside down on either final page.

Goals: 1. *Phonology*
Reduce final consonant deletion (FCD)
Reduce deaffrication
Reduce depalatalization
Produce /ʤ/
Produce /l/
Produce /ʃ/
Produce /b/
Produce /d/ and /t/
Produce /k/

2. *Syntax*
Comprehend and use verb forms (irregular past)
Comprehend and use morphological forms (articles)
Comprehend and use pronouns

3. *Semantics*
Comprehend and use spatial concepts
(backwards, upside down)

4. *Thinking Skills*
Predict events
Detect and explain absurdities

Themes: People (occupations)
Places

Additional Activities: 1. Read additional books:
King Bidgood's in the Bathtub (1985)
by Audrey Wood
New York: Harcourt Brace

Description: A fun-loving king refuses to get out of the bathtub to rule his kingdom. The

entire court fails to persuade him to leave his tub. A royal page ends up solving the problem.

Down by the Bay (1999)
by Raffi
New York: Crown

Description: Down by the bay, two young friends make up fantastic rhymes about animals.

2. Have children put their initials on the states they have visited on a copy of a U.S. map. Talk about some of the famous landmarks children have seen in various states. Have them bring in photographs from home to help them talk about their sightseeing.

3. Play with words by having children make alliterations to go with their name (e.g., Active Andrew, Kind Kate, Angelic Anna, Marvelous Matthew). Duplicate a blank title page by covering up the picture and the title on an existing title page. Have children use the blank title pages to create a personalized pattern book using their alliterative names.

4. Explain your occupation to children and then have them name an occupation that they might like to do when they grow up. Help them determine what they will need to do to get the job by starting with the overall goal and working their way down to the immediate tasks (e.g., graduate from college with a degree in that field, graduate from high school, pass fourth grade, earn good grades, study for tests, listen during class, learn the alphabet).

Jolly
Joshua

by _____

What a silly way to walk—

backwards, upside down!

Jolly Joshua went to

_____,

(place)

walking backwards,

upside down. On the

way, he met

_____.

(person)

Jolly Joshua went to

_____,

(place)

walking backwards,

upside down. On the

way, he met

_____.

(person)

Showy Shelly

by _____

What a silly way to walk—

backwards, upside down!

Showy Shelly went to

_____,
(place)

walking backwards, upside down. On the way, she met

_____.
(person)

Showy Shelly went to

_____,
(place)

walking backwards, upside down. On the way, she met

_____.
(person)

the Statue of Liberty

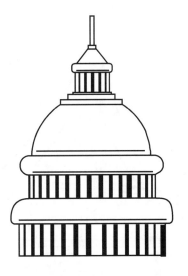

the U.S. Capitol building

the Grand Canyon

Mount Rushmore

the Golden Gate Bridge

the Rocky Mountains

Disneyland

the Alamo

a judge

a construction worker

a cashier

an electrician

271

a beautician

a grocer

a banker

a teacher

Kid's Day

Model Story: ***Cookie's Week*** (1997)
by Cindy Ward
New York: Putnam

Description: This sweet and simple tale chronicles how Cookie the cat gets into a different kind of mischief every day of the week. This is a 32-page book.

Predictable Pattern: At school, I played with _____. They (objects)

were everywhere!

Notes: Children can complete the predictable pattern with the name of an object. The final page is on the bottom half of page 276. On the final page, children can draw a picture of how the toys and other materials look after they have been cleaned up.

Goals: 1. *Phonology*
Reduce fronting
Reduce stopping
Reduce vocalization
Reduce cluster simplification (CS)
Produce /s/
Produce /p/
Produce /k/
Produce semivowel /r/
Produce /θ/ and /ð/
Produce /l/

2. *Syntax*

Comprehend and use verb forms (past, copula)

Comprehend and use sentence structures (complex)

Comprehend and use morphological forms (plurals)

Comprehend and use pronouns

3. *Semantics*

Comprehend and use spatial concepts (everywhere)

4. *Thinking Skills*

Make associations

Establish causality

Categorize objects

Themes: Toys

School

Additional Activities:

1. Read an additional book:

Suddenly! (1998)

by Colin McNaughton

New York: Voyager Picture Books

Description: Each time a wolf tries to capture a piglet who is on his way home from school, the piglet suddenly changes his course.

2. Have children write a description and/or draw a picture of their favorite toy or book. Pair up children and have them tell each other about their descriptions and/or pictures.

3. Have children learn or recite the days of the week and the months of the year. To aid recall, make visual and gestural associations with each day and/or month (e.g., clasp your hands over your head to make a sun for *Sunday,* march in place for *March).*

4. Create a pattern book using the routines of the school day. Use predictable patterns, such as:

This week at school, I _____.
Before school, I _____.
As I come into school, I _____.
Before lunch, I _____.
After lunch, I _____.
After computer time, I _____.
Before circle time, I _____.
At the end of the day, I _____.

Use these sentences to create original pattern books that children can illustrate. Have children complete the blanks with appropriate activities.

5. Ask children temporal questions, such as:

"Which comes first, getting on the bus or eating lunch?"

"What do you usually do last, brush your teeth or eat breakfast?"

"Which comes first, taking a bath or going to bed?"

"What do you do last, put on your coat or zip your coat?"

Kid's Day

by _____

When I'm all done playing with my toys,

I have to clean up.

**At school,
I played with**

_____.

(objects)

**They were

everywhere!**

**At school,
I played with**

_____.

(objects)

**They were

everywhere!**

© 2000 Thinking Publications

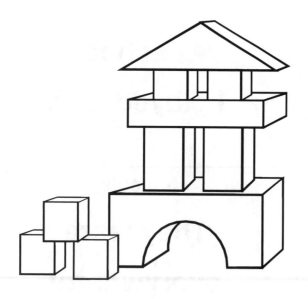

blocks

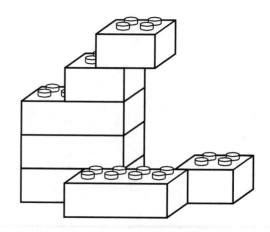

LEGOS

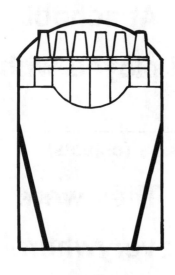

crayons

dolls

books

puzzles

cards

cars

My Pet Dog
My Pet Cat

Model Story: ***The Judge*** (1988)

by Harve Zemach

New York: Farrar, Straus and Giroux

Description: This 48-page book uses repetitive rhyme sets to describe a horrible creature. The judge, however, does not believe that anyone really saw the creature.

Predictable Patterns:

Dog: Its eyes are black. It has fur on its _____. Its paws
      (rhyming word)

have claws. It snaps its _____. It growls and groans.
                        (rhyming word)

It chews up _____. It creeps in the dark, without a
           (rhyming word)

_____. It likes to eat, a shoe and a _____. It is
(rhyming word)   (rhyming word)

quite tame. It has a _____. It's my _____,
                     (rhyming word)   (animal)

_____.
(animal's name)

Cat: It can hiss and purr. It cleans its _____. It creeps in the
                                          (rhyming word)

night. It keeps out of _____. It likes to have fun. It
                       (rhyming word)

sleeps in the _____. It is quite tame. It has a _____.
              (rhyming word)   (rhyming word)

It's my _____, _____.
        (animal) (animal's name)

Notes: Two different pattern books are provided—*My Pet Dog* and *My Pet Cat*. Children should complete each predictable pattern with a rhyming word. The *My Pet Dog* book can have up to eight pages. The title page and final page for *My Pet Dog* are on page 283, the pattern pages are on pages 284–286, and the corresponding illustrations are on pages 287–288. On the final page, children can draw a picture of their real pet dog or a dog they might wish to own.

My Pet Cat can have up to six pages. The title page and final page for *My Pet Cat* are on page 289, the pattern pages are on pages 290–291, and the corresponding illustrations are on pages 292. On the final page, children can draw a picture of their real pet cat or a cat they might wish to own.

Goals: 1. *Phonology*
Reduce final consonant deletion (FCD)
Reduce cluster simplification (CS)
Reduce assimilation
Produce /s/
Produce /k/ and /g/
Produce /r/
Produce /l/

2. *Syntax*
Comprehend and use verb forms
    (present, copula, infinitive)
Comprehend and use morphological forms
    (articles, possessives, plurals)
Comprehend and use pronouns

3. *Semantics*
Comprehend and use quality concepts (descriptors)
Comprehend and use spatial concepts (on)

4. *Thinking Skills*
Make associations
Draw inferences

Themes: Animals (pets)
Rhymes
Actions

Additional Activities:

1. Read an additional book:
   World's Weirdest Reptiles (1994)
   by M.L. Roberts
   New York: Troll

   Description: Unusual but real reptiles from all over the world are described and shown in vivid photographs.

2. Help children generate rhyming word pairs that describe a variety of animals. Name an animal and have a child give a word that describes the animal. Then have another child give a word that rhymes with the descriptive word (e.g., "Rabbit"..."Furry"... "Hurry"). Write the rhymes on large sheets of paper and display them where everyone can see them. Children can then make original rhyming verses about their favorite animals.

3. Incorporate strategies that provide visual, auditory, and kinesthetic cues to help children recall the descriptive phrases in the model story—*The Judge.* Use gestures for each descriptive line as children say each trait they see (e.g., while saying, "Its eyes are black. It has fur on its back," point to your eyes and touch your back). In addition, use multiple repetitions to help children recall the traits of the cumulative description.

4. The story *The Judge* makes a great classroom play for children of all ability levels to perform. Children can have the opportunity to construct sets, create and wear costumes, learn parts, take turns, work cooperatively, and perform in front of a group.

My Pet Dog

by _____

It's my _____, _____.
              (animal)   **(animal's name)**

© 2000 Thinking Publications

Its eyes are black.

It has fur on its

_____.

(rhyming word)

Its paws have claws.

It snaps its

_____.

(rhyming word)

284

It growls
and groans.
It chews up

_____.

(rhyming word)

It creeps in the dark,

without a

_____.

(rhyming word)

It likes to eat,
a shoe and a

_____.
(rhyming word)

It is quite tame.
It has a

_____.
(rhyming word)

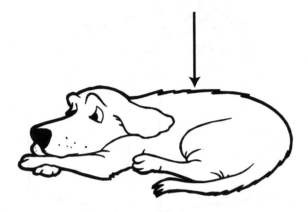

back

jaws

bones

bark

treat   **name**

My Pet Cat

by _____

It's my _____, _____.
  (animal)   (animal's name)

It can hiss and purr.

It cleans its

_____.

(rhyming word)

It creeps in the night.

It keeps out of

_____.

(rhyming word)

It likes to have fun.

It sleeps in the

_____.

(rhyming word)

It is quite tame.

It has a

_____.

(rhyming word)

fur

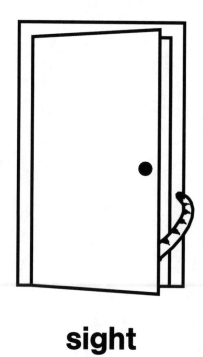

sight

sun

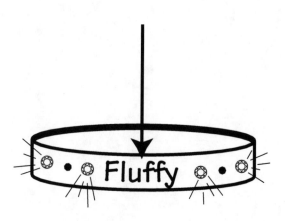

name

STORY PROFILE

One Bright Fall Morning

Model Story: *One Bright Monday Morning* (1962)
by Arline and Joseph Baum
New York: Random House

NOTE: This book is out of print, but it might still be located in local and school libraries.

Description: In this book, a fall theme is used as the setting for repetitive verse and counting.

Predictable Pattern: One _____ _____ morning, while on my way
              (descriptor) (day of the week)

to school, I saw _____ _____ _____.
                    (number)   (object)   (action)

Notes: Children should complete the predictable pattern with a descriptor, a day of the week, and an activity description (number, object, action). This pattern book will contain nine pages when completed (i.e., a title page, one pattern page for each day of the week, and a final page). The title page and final page are on page 296. Children can draw a fall scene on the final page. The pattern pages for Monday through Friday are on page 297, and the pattern pages for Saturday and Sunday are on page 298. The activity illustrations for the pattern pages are on pages 299–302. Children can illustrate the various types of weather on each page or use the weather/day illustrations that are provided on pages 299–300. When students are using two photocopied illustrations per page, the pictures should be glued side by side.

Goals: 1. *Phonology*
　　　Reduce vocalization
　　　Reduce cluster simplification (CS)
　　　Produce semivowels /r/ and /l/
　　　Produce /s/

　　2. *Syntax*
　　　Comprehend and use verb forms
　　　　(irregular past, participle)
　　　Comprehend and use sentence structures (complex)
　　　Comprehend and use morphological forms (plurals)
　　　Comprehend and use pronouns

　　3. *Semantics*
　　　Comprehend and use time concepts
　　　　(days of the week)
　　　Comprehend and use quantity concepts (numbers)
　　　Comprehend and use quality concepts (descriptors)

　　4. *Thinking Skills*
　　　Predict events
　　　Draw inferences
　　　Sequence events or objects

Themes: Nature
　　　Time (seasons)
　　　Counting

Additional Activities: 1. Read additional books:
　　　When Autumn Comes (1992)
　　　by Robert Maass
　　　New York: Owlet

　　　Description: Beautifully composed color photos
　　　　　　　　are combined with a brief text to
　　　　　　　　portray typical events of autumn.

　　　Red Leaf, Yellow Leaf (1991)
　　　by Lois Ehlert
　　　New York: Harcourt Brace

Description: A child describes the growth of a maple tree from seed to sapling.

2. For a writing lesson, extend the end of each predictable pattern by writing, "because _____" on the bottom of each page where the text ends. Encourage children to complete each sentence by writing a reason for the action.

3. While conducting a unit on seasons, make a chart of opposites. Contrast fall to spring, and winter to summer in regard to the weather, seasonal activities, daylight hours, clothing worn, and position of the earth in relation to the sun. Use seasonal words and pictures to fill in the chart.

4. Consider having children use several copies of the pattern pages from page 297–298 as a daily journal. Keep the pages accessible to children to complete on a daily basis. After several weeks worth of pages have been completed, look back through all the entries and talk about how the weather changed.

One Bright Fall Morning

by _____

It's fall!

One

_____
(descriptor)

_____
(day of the week)

morning, while on my way to school, I saw

_____ _____ _____.
(number)   (object)   (action)

One

_____
(descriptor)

_____
(day of the week)

morning, while on my way to school, I saw

_____ _____ _____.
(number)   (object)   (action)

One

_____
(descriptor)

_____
(day of the week)

morning, while raking leaves in my yard, I saw

_____ _____ _____.
(number) **(object)** **(action)**

One

_____
(descriptor)

_____
(day of the week)

morning, while driving with my family, I saw

_____ _____ _____.
(number) **(object)** **(action)**

dark Monday

foggy Tuesday

windy Wednesday

rainy Thursday

chilly Friday

cloudy Saturday

bright Sunday

1 sun rising

2 bushes turning colors

3 children playing soccer

4 leaves falling down

© 2000 Thinking Publications

5 children
wearing costumes

6 geese
flying south

7 farmers
harvesting apples

302

STORY PROFILE

Stanley Gets Ready for School!

Model Story: *Froggy Gets Dressed* (1997)
by Jonathan London
New York: Viking

Description: Using questions, alliteration, and onomatopoeia, this humorous, 32-page story is a dialogue between a mother frog and her son about the important clothing to put on when getting ready to play in the snow.

**Predictable
Pattern:**   "Stanley," said Mother.

"What?" asked Stanley.

"Did you forget something?"

Stanley thought.

Then he ran upstairs—step, step, step.

He came downstairs—stomp, stomp, jump.

He put his _____ in his backpack, z-z-z-zip!
           (object)

Notes: Children can complete the predictable pattern with an object. The final page to the story is on the bottom half of page 306. Children can draw a picture of Stanley hurrying out to catch the school bus on that page.

Goals: 1. *Phonology*

   Reduce fronting

   Reduce gliding

   Reduce stopping

   Reduce cluster simplification (CS)

   Reduce final consonant deletion (FCD)

   Produce /s/ and /z/

Produce /θ/ and /ð/
Produce /f/
Produce /k/
Produce /d/ and /t/
Produce /l/

2. *Syntax*

Comprehend and use question forms (what, yes/no)
Comprehend and use verb forms
   (irregular past)
Comprehend and use morphological forms
   (articles, plurals)
Comprehend and use pronouns

3. *Semantics*

Comprehend and use spatial concepts (up, down)
Comprehend and use time concepts (morning)

4. *Thinking Skills*

Predict events
Establish causality
Sequence events or objects

Theme: School

Additional Activities:

1. Read an additional book:

   Froggy Learns to Swim (1997)
   by Jonathan London
   New York: Puffin

   Description: Froggy's mother teaches him how to swim while exchanging dialogue containing questions, answers, and onomatopoeia.

2. Have a problem-solving class discussion about ways Froggy could improve his chaotic morning. Suggest problems that might have occurred because of Froggy's lack of organization when getting ready for school. Figure out a sequential plan for the night

before or a morning routine that might have helped Froggy. Have children list and/or illustrate a set of steps they might use to get ready for school. Consider using a timeline graphic or another visual tool to help children list the steps.

3. Have children use multiple modalities while learning and telling the story; they will have an easier time recalling the lengthy predictable pattern. Have children look at the pictures, say the predictable pattern aloud, and pantomime the gestures (e.g., going up and down stairs, cupping their hands around their mouth while yelling, zipping their coat). Have children pair up with a partner, each take a character part, and retell the story.

4. Create an interactive language chart using the sentences in the framed box below. Refer to the procedures provided in Appendix H (page 379) for creating and using an interactive language chart.

> Froggy, Froggy, do your best.
>
> Froggy, Froggy, go get dressed.
>
> Put on your _____.
>   (object)
>
> Zip, zup, zat.

Alternate between clothing and nonclothing items to complete the blank so that students can catch the absurdities in some of the choices while reciting the pattern.

Stanley Gets Ready for School!

by _____

"Stanley," said Mother.

"What?" asked Stanley.

"Did you forget something?"

Stanley looked out the window.

The school bus was outside—NOW!

"Stanley," said Mother.

"What?" asked Stanley.

"Did you forget something?"

Stanley thought. Then he ran

upstairs—step, step, step.

He came downstairs—

stomp, stomp, jump.

He put his _____
                    (object)

in his backpack, z-z-z-zip!

"Stanley," said Mother.

"What?" asked Stanley.

"Did you forget something?"

Stanley thought. Then he ran

upstairs—step, step, step.

He came downstairs—

stomp, stomp, jump.

He put his _____
                    (object)

in his backpack, z-z-z-zip!

library book

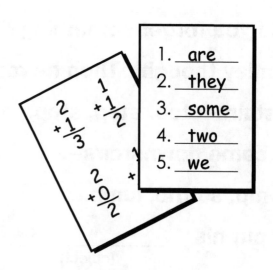

pencil

Froggy has my permission to go on the field trip.

Mrs. Johnson

permission slip

homework

lunch ticket

gym shoes

jacket

show-and-tell toy

STORY PROFILE

Time for Spring!

Model Story: ***Time to Sleep*** (1997)
by Denise Fleming
New York: Holt

Description: This 32-page story revolves around various woodland animals noticing the signs of winter, which brings hibernation time to the forest.

Predictable Pattern: The _____ says, "I see spring in the air. It's time to
(animal or person)

_____, but first I must tell _____."
(action)   (animal or person)

Notes: As in the model book, the last animal name on each pattern page is the name of the animal that appears on the following page. On the last pattern page, children should write their name on the last blank line of the predictable pattern. Suggested responses for the actions that children could place in the second blank line of the predictable pattern are listed below:

bird—build a nest
worm—tunnel dirt
bee—gather pollen
butterfly—come out of my cocoon
bear—come out of my cave
ant—crawl up a tree stump
goose—fly north
farmer—plant crops

The title page and final page are on page 313. Children can draw a picture of what they like to do in spring on the last page.

Goals: 1. *Phonology*
Reduce cluster simplification (CS)
Reduce stopping
Reduce vocalization
Produce /s/
Produce semivowels /r/ and /l/
Produce /f/

2. *Syntax*
Comprehend and use verb forms
(present, infinitive, modal)
Comprehend and use sentence structures (compound)
Comprehend and use pronouns

3. *Semantics*
Comprehend and use time concepts (seasons)

4. *Thinking Skills*
Make associations
Predict events
Establish causality

Themes: Nature
Animals
Time (seasons)
Actions

Additional Activities:

1. Read an additional book:
Animals in Winter (1999)
by Henrietta Bancroft and Richard G. Van Gelder
New York: HarperCollins

Description: This book describes how animals cope with winter, including migration, hibernation, and food storage.

2. Use the predictable pattern from the pattern story incorporating other senses. Have each student say,

"I _____ spring in the air. It's time to
(sense)

_____, but first I must tell _____."
(spring activity)   (another student's name)

Encourage and model descriptions that tap into modalities other than sight (e.g., "I smell spring in the air. It's time to plant flowers, but first I must tell Emma").

3. Talk about how the plan in the story's predictable pattern is not listed in the sequence it should be completed. Give a variety of examples, such as,

"Class, line up for lunch, but first clear your desks and wash your hands. Which activity are you supposed to do first? Second? Last?"

"Raise your hand if you're ready to color your picture, but first throw your scraps in the garbage. What are you supposed to do first? Second?"

"Make sure you get a drink of water before you return to class, but first use the bathroom to wash your hands. What are you supposed to do first? Second? Third?"

4. Sharpen listening skills by playing a memory game. Children can take turns naming signs of winter, spring, summer, or fall after repeating all previously mentioned signs. For example, one student might start by saying, "Cool weather is a sign of fall." The next student might then say, "Cool weather and leaves changing colors are signs of fall." Then a third student might say, "Cool weather, leaves changing colors, and school starting are signs of fall."

5. As an authentic assessment instrument, children can make charts depicting signs of seasonal changes. For each child, divide a piece of paper into four equal parts and label each section with a season name. Direct children to draw or write about one season in each area of the paper. Children's entries can pertain to seasonal changes or how each season affects them personally.

Time for Spring!

by _____

It's spring, and I want to _____.

(activity)

The _____ says,
(animal or person)

"I see spring in the air.

It's time to _____,
(action)

but first I must tell

_____."
(animal or person)

The _____ says,
(animal or person)

"I see spring in the air.

It's time to _____,
(action)

but first I must tell

_____."
(animal or person)

314

bird

worm

bee

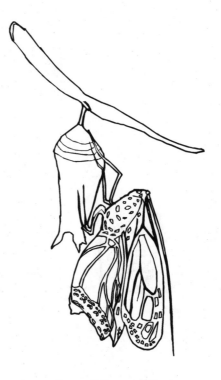

butterfly

315

bear

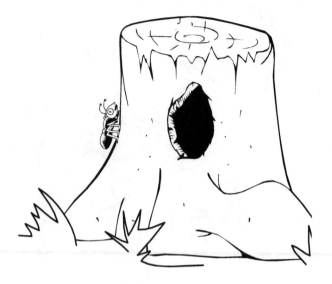

ant

goose

farmer

316

To the Zoo We'll Go
A-Riding We Will Go
A-Shopping We Will Go

Model Story: ***Oh, A-Hunting We Will Go*** (1991)
by John Langstaff
New York: Aladdin

Description: This 32-page book tells old and new verses to a popular folk song about hunting and capturing an animal and then letting it go.

Predictable Patterns:

To the Zoo: Oh, to the zoo we'll go. Oh, to the zoo we'll go.

We'll see _____ _____.
        (animal)   (rhyming action)

And then we'll all go home.

A-Riding: Oh, a-riding we will go. Oh, a-riding we will go.

We'll ride in _____ and see _____.
          (vehicle)   (rhyming object)

And then we'll all go home.

A-Shopping: Oh, a-shopping we will go. Oh, a-shopping we will go.

We'll see _____ and buy _____.
        (object)   (rhyming clothing)

And then we'll all go home.

Notes: Three different pattern books are provided for this model story. Children can complete the *To the Zoo We'll Go* predictable pattern with an animal and a rhyming item. The title page and final page are on page 321, the pattern pages are on page 322, and the illustrations are on pages 323–324.

Children can complete the *A-Riding We Will Go* predictable pattern with a vehicle and a rhyming word. The title page and final page are on page 325, the pattern pages are on page 326, and the illustrations are on pages 327–328.

Children can complete the *A-Shopping We Will Go* predictable pattern with an object and a rhyming clothing item. The title page and final page are on page 329, the pattern pages are on page 330, and the illustrations are on pages 331–332.

On the final pages, children can draw a picture of themselves traveling home from their journey or make up their own rhyme to fit the theme.

Goals: 1. *Phonology*
Reduce fronting
Reduce gliding
Reduce depalatalization
Reduce stopping
Reduce vocalization
Produce /s/ and /z/
Produce /ð/
Produce /g/
Produce /ʃ/
Produce semivowel /l/
Produce /r/

2. *Syntax*
Comprehend and use verb forms
    (present progressive, future, copula)
Comprehend and use sentence structures (compound)
Comprehend and use morphological forms (articles)
Comprehend and use pronouns

3. *Semantics*
Comprehend and use spatial concepts
    (in, below, over, under)

4. *Thinking Skills*
   Sequence events or objects
   Categorize objects

Themes: Animals (zoo)
Transportation
Places (shopping)
Rhymes

Additional Activities:

1. Read an additional book:
   I Can't Said the Ant (1961)
   by Polly Cameron
   New York: Putnam

   Description: This book is a rebus story with kitchen foods and objects speaking in rhyme about how to mend a broken teapot and have the ant put it back in its place.

2. Use blank index cards to make rhyming decks using any or all of the three themes (i.e., zoo, transportation, shopping). Write one word (paired with a corresponding picture, if necessary) on each card, being sure to include at least two words from each desired rhyme family. Use the deck(s) during activity centers to play traditional matching games (e.g., Go Fish, Memory, Old Maid). Some possible rhyming-word sets to use include:

   Zoo: *zoo—blue*
   bear—hair
   whale—tail
   fox—box
   ape—grape
   snake—rake

   Transportation: *car—star*
   van—pan
   sled—bed

truck—duck
plane—train
go-cart—heart
jeep—sheep
hot-air balloon—moon

Shopping: *money—honey*
toy—boy
store—door
pay—day
dollar—holler
dime—time
nickel—pickle
shop—hop
cart—dart

3. Sing the zoo pattern to children using a variety of animal names, but make sure the final word in the pattern does not rhyme with the animal name (e.g., "We'll see a cow kicking a can"). Have children change the final word so that it rhymes with the animal name. Then have children sing the new rhyming verse.

4. Extend the shopping theme to include additional categories (e.g., toys, food, pets, vehicles). Provide pictures from each category, mix them up, and have students sort the items into the designated categories.

5. Provide auditory, visual, and kinesthetic cues to children to help them learn the rhyming verses in the pattern books. For example, say the rhyming words louder than the rest of the sentence, repeat the rhyming words several times, point to pictures of the words when saying the rhyme, and have children perform an action for each rhyming word (e.g., circling their eyes for "seeing," steering for "riding").

To the Zoo We'll Go

by _____

And then we'll all go home!

    © 2000 Thinking Publications

Oh, to the zoo we'll go.

Oh, to the zoo we'll go.

We'll see _____
(animal)

_____.
(rhyming action)

And then we'll all go home.

Oh, to the zoo we'll go.

Oh, to the zoo we'll go.

We'll see _____
(animal)

_____.
(rhyming action)

And then we'll all go home.

a bear

combing its hair

a fish

making a wish

a bat

flying below a hat

a snake

swimming in a lake

323

a crocodile

running a mile

llamas

wearing pajamas

a peacock

**dancing under
a clock**

a toad

jumping over a road

A-Riding We Will Go

by _____

And then we'll all go home!

Oh, a-riding we will go.

Oh, a-riding we will go.

We'll ride in _____
                         (vehicle)

and see _____.
                    (rhyming object)

And then we'll all go home.

Oh, a-riding we will go.

Oh, a-riding we will go.

We'll ride in _____
                         (vehicle)

and see _____.
                    (rhyming object)

And then we'll all go home.

a car

a van

a star

a fan

a sled

a truck

a bed

a duck

a plane

a go-cart

a train

a heart

a jeep

a hot-air balloon

a sheep

the moon

328

A-Shopping We Will Go

by _____

And then we'll all go home!

© 2000 Thinking Publications

Oh, a-shopping we will go.

Oh, a-shopping we will go.

We'll see _____
(object)

and buy _____.
(rhyming clothing)

And then we'll all go home.

Oh, a-shopping we will go.

Oh, a-shopping we will go.

We'll see _____
(object)

and buy _____.
(rhyming clothing)

And then we'll all go home.

a cat

a hat

some ants

some pants

a goat

a coat

a clock

a sock

331
© 2000 Thinking Publications

some roots   some glue

some boots   a shoe

a pear   a pile of dirt

underwear   a shirt

332

STORY PROFILE

The Very Hungry Bear

Model Story: *The Very Hungry Caterpillar* (1994)
by Eric Carle
New York: Philomel Books

Description: In this 28-page book, a caterpillar eats its way through various foods, increasing the number of items each day of the week. The pages contain holes where the caterpillar has eaten through them.

Predictable Pattern: The very hungry bear ate _____ _____, but he
(number)   (food)

was still hungry.

Notes: Children should complete each predictable pattern with both the quantity and name of each snack. The final page is on the bottom half of page 336. Children can draw a picture of a bear hibernating on that page.

Goals: 1. *Phonology*
Reduce gliding
Reduce vocalization
Reduce final consonant deletion (FCD)
Produce /r/ and semivowel /r/
Produce /b/
Produce /tʃ/
Produce /l/
Produce /t/

2. *Syntax*
Comprehend and use verb forms (irregular past)
Comprehend and use sentence structures (compound)

Comprehend and use morphological forms (plurals)

Comprehend and use pronouns

3. *Semantics*

Comprehend and use quantity concepts (numbers)

4. *Thinking Skills*

Predict events

Sequence events or objects

Establish causality

Themes: Counting

Animals (bears)

Food

Additional Activities:

1. Read additional books:

There Was an Old Lady Who Swallowed a Fly

(1997)

by Simms Taback

New York: Viking

Description: This book is based on the old song about a woman who kept swallowing larger and larger animals but succumbed after eating a horse.

Snake Supper (1995)

by Alan Durant

New York: Golden Books

Description: A hungry snake slithers through the forest swallowing up bigger and bigger animals for supper until he meets a clever elephant who outwits him.

2. Use *Snake Supper* to create a pattern book called *Rosie's Breakfast*. Use the following predictable pattern on the pages in the book:

I'm hungry! Rosie saw something _____.

(shape)

She opened her mouth wider and swallowed

_____, *but she was still hungry!*
(food)

Complete the first blank with a shape and the second blank with a food that has that shape. Ideas for food pictures include an orange, a piece of toast, a banana, a bowl of cereal, two bacon strips, three eggs, a stack of pancakes, and a gallon of milk.

3. Make a caterpillar sock puppet. Cut food patterns from poster board to match items mentioned in *The Very Hungry Caterpillar*. Make the patterns large enough so that a hole can be made through the middle of each piece of food, and the sock puppet can fit through the hole. Have the caterpillar eat its way through each piece of food as children retell the story.

4. Discuss the many types of bears that exist (e.g., brown bear, polar bear, panda bear, koala bear, teddy bear). List the names of the bears and have children draw or locate pictures of the various bears. (Use the bears on pages 97–98, if desired.) Talk about how the various bears are alike and different.

5. Introduce four basic food groups (breads, meats, fruits and vegetables, dairy) and write the name of each group on a separate piece of poster board. Have children cut pictures of foods from magazines and glue each picture onto the appropriate piece of poster board to make four collages. Display the collages in a prominent location.

6. Bring in a clear storage bag filled with food items (e.g., grapes, baby carrots, small crackers). Divide children into two groups. Have one group estimate the number of items in the bag. Have the other group count the items. Talk about how the estimation compared to the actual number.

The Very Hungry Bear

by _____

When he finished eating, the bear laid down to take a long winter's nap, called hibernation.

**The very hungry
bear ate**

_____ _____,
(number)   (food)

**but he was still
hungry.**

**The very hungry
bear ate**

_____ _____,
(number)   (food)

**but he was still
hungry.**

337

1

fish

2

hives of honey

3

cherries

4

sandwiches

338

5

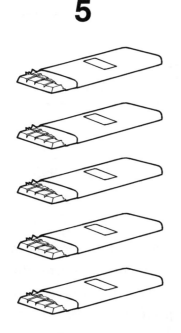

chocolate bars

6

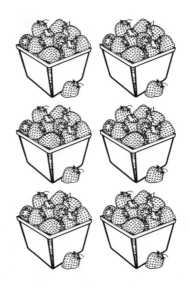

batches of strawberries

7

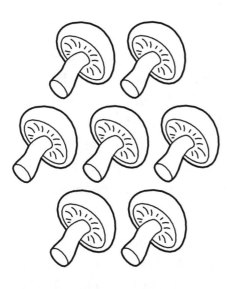

mushrooms

8

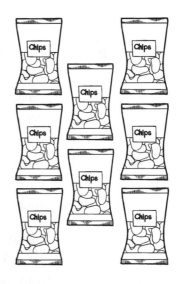

bags of chips

STORY PROFILES

Who Walks in the Zoo at Night?
Who Moves in the Forest at Night?

Model Story: *Who Walks on This Halloween Night?* (1998)
by Harriet Ziefert
New York: Little Simon

Description: This 16-page book uses rhyme and alliteration in its question-and-answer format. Answers are hidden behind a flap portion of the page, allowing children a chance to predict an appropriate response.

Predictable Patterns:

Zoo: Who walks _____ _____ in the zoo at
        (sound)   (sound)

night? A _____ _____!
          (participle)   (animal)

Forest: Who moves in the forest at night?

A _____ _____!
   (participle)   (animal)

Notes: Two different pattern books are provided for this pattern story. Children should complete the predictable pattern for *Who Walks in the Zoo at Night?* with two sounds, a participle, and an animal. The title page and final page are on page 343, the pattern pages are on page 344, and the illustrations are on pages 345–346. Children can draw a picture of a zookeeper on the final page.

Children should complete the predictable pattern for *Who Moves in the Forest at Night?* with a participle and an animal. The title page and final page for for the forest book are on page 347, the pattern pages are on page 348, and the illustrations are on pages 349–350. Children can draw a picture of a camper on the final page.

Goals: 1. *Phonology*
Reduce stopping
Reduce final consonant deletion (FCD)
Reduce cluster simplification (CS)
Produce /s/ and /z/
Produce /f/ and /v/
Produce /t/

2. *Syntax*
Comprehend and use verb forms
    (present, participle, infinitive)
Comprehend and use questions (who)
Comprehend and use morphological forms (articles)

3. *Semantics*
Comprehend and use time concepts (night)
Comprehend and use spatial concepts (in)
Comprehend and use quality concepts (descriptors)

4. *Thinking Skills*
Categorize objects

Themes: Animals (zoo, forest)
Rhymes

**Additional
Activities:** 1. Read an additional book:
On Our Way to the Forest! (1993)
by Harriet Ziefert
New York: HarperCollins

Description: Come and see all the noisy forest animals as they romp through the woods.

2. Compare the number of syllables in the animal's names (e.g., "*Elephant* has three parts"). Have

children clap out the syllables they hear as they say each animal's name.

3. If children are having difficulty with the targeted "participle + animal" response at the bottom of each pattern page (e.g., "A jumping kangaroo"), simplify the response by changing the pattern (e.g., "A <u>kangaroo</u> jumps in the zoo!").

4. Have children make the sounds and perform the actions of each illustrated animal. Take turns having children describe what they are doing as they perform the actions (e.g., as children make monkey sounds and actions, say something like "Monkeys chitter, chatter; climb trees; and swing their arms").

Who Walks in the Zoo at Night?

by _____

After checking all the animals at night, who yawns and goes to sleep?

The zookeeper!

Who walks _____ _____
                        (sound)   (sound)

in the zoo at night?

A _____
            (participle)

_____!
      (animal)

Who walks _____ _____
                        (sound)   (sound)

in the zoo at night?

A _____
            (participle)

_____!
      (animal)

stamp, stomp

stomping elephant

clip, clop

grazing zebra

pitter, patter

pacing tiger

hip, hop

jumping kangaroo

swish, swoosh

prancing ostrich

chitter, chatter

climbing monkey

widdle, waddle

toddling penguin

scritch, scratch

creeping cricket

Who Moves in the Forest at Night?

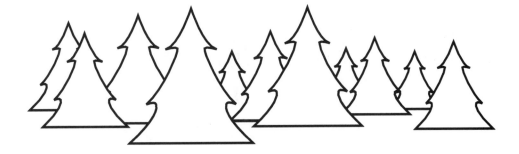

by _____

After hearing all the animals at night, who yawns and goes to sleep?

A camper!

Who moves in the forest at night?

A _____ _____!
   (participle)   **(animal)**

Who moves in the forest at night?

A _____ _____!
   (participle)   **(animal)**

running raccoon

flapping firefly

hopping frog

buzzing bee

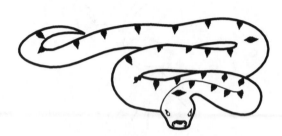

slithering snake

prancing deer

**wandering
woodchuck**

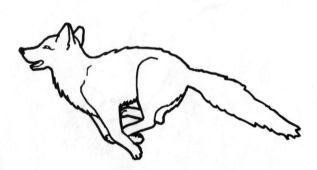

frolicking fox

STORY PROFILE

Zicka Zicka Zoom Zoom!

Model Story: ***Chicka Chicka Boom Boom*** (1989)
by Bill Martin, Jr., and John Archambault
New York: Simon and Schuster

Description: This 40-page book captivates children with rhythm and rhyme. Upper- and lowercase alphabet letters climb their way up a coconut tree and explore what might happen.

Predictable Pattern: Zicka zicka zoom zoom!
Will there be enough room?
Here comes _____ up the tropical tree.
(sound or insect)

Notes: There are two versions of this pattern story—sounds and insects. For a sounds book, have children complete the predictable pattern with a sound. The pattern pages are on page 355, and 12 T-shirt illustrations are provided on pages 356–358. Eight of the T-shirts have sound names printed on them. Four are blank so that the names of any sounds (including vowels or consonants) children are learning can be inserted. Have students use their thumbprints to create creature heads above the T-shirts and then have them add head and body details.

For an insect book, have children complete the predictable pattern with an insect name. The pattern pages are on page 355, and the illustrations are on pages 359–360. The bottom half of page 354 is to be inserted every 3 or 4 pages and is also to be used as the final page for either book.

Goals: 1. *Phonology*
Produce any consonant phoneme
Reduce any phonological process

2. *Syntax*
Comprehend and use question forms (yes/no)
Comprehend and use verb forms (present, future)
Comprehend and use morphological forms (articles)

3. *Semantics*
Comprehend and use spatial concepts (up)

4. *Thinking Skills*
Make associations
Predict events

Themes: School (alphabet)
Animals (insects)
Rhymes
Imagination (monsters)

Additional Activities:

1. Read an additional book:
Wacky Wednesday (1974)
by Theodore LeSieg
New York: Random House

Description: Drawings and verse point out the many things that are wrong one wacky Wednesday.

2. Create an interactive language chart using the sentences in the framed box below. Refer to the procedures provided in Appendix H (page 379) for creating and using an interactive language chart.

> Zicka zicka zoom zoom!
>
> Will there be enough room?
>
> Here comes _____ up the tropical tree.
>   (sound or insect)

(Children's names could also be inserted in the blank.)

3. Combine two or three syllables to make nonsense words (e.g., *bata, pakada, mataba)*. Have children clap out the number of syllables they hear in each nonsense word. Then have children say or write another nonsense word with an equal number of syllables. Children can make another pattern book using the nonsense words they created on the pattern pages from this story.

4. On a long strip of paper, have students write the animal names (or draw pictures) that could go up and down the tropical tree. Have everyone sing the first two lines of the predictable pattern (i.e., "Zicka zicka zoom zoom! Will there be enough room?"). Then ask one child to respond with the animal that is next on the list by singing, "Here comes _____ (animal name) up the tropical tree." (For older children, list the animals in alphabetical order.)

5. Make a sound wheel for students to use to practice blending and segmenting sounds. Cut two identical circles from heavy stock paper (approximately 8" in diameter). Cut 8, 1" × ½" rectangular windows in a circular fashion on one circle (see sample below for placement of the windows). Write a consonant sound to precede each window. Line up the circles and fasten them together with a brad. Write one rime in each window (e.g., *at, ed, et, ad, ot, ug, ock, and, ear, ate)*. Have children rotate the circles while creating and saying new word combinations.

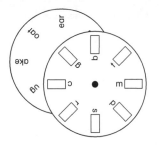 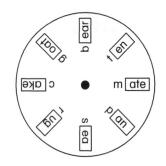

Zicka Zicka Zoom Zoom!

by _____

Zicka zicka zoom zoom!

354

Zicka zicka zoom zoom!

Will there be enough room?

Here comes _____

(sound or insect)

up the tropical tree.

Zicka zicka zoom zoom!

Will there be enough room?

Here comes _____

(sound or insect)

up the tropical tree.

B Creature

M Creature

P Creature

T Creature

356

D Creature

N Creature

C Creature

G Creature

357

_____ **Creature**   _____ **Creature**

_____ **Creature**   _____ **Creature**

358

a cricket

a fly

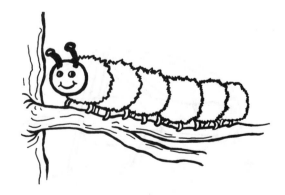

a caterpillar

a ladybug

an ant

a bee

a spider

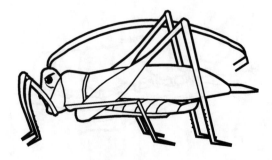

a grasshopper

APPENDICES

More Story Making!
Procedures Outline

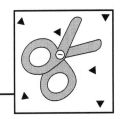

1. Choose a pattern book based on children's goals by using the cross-reference charts on pages 46–57.

2. Read the story profile and gather the model story the pattern book is based on. (Refer to Table 5 on pages 28–31 to find the model story that corresponds to the pattern book.)

3. Prepare materials.

4. Read the model story.

5. When using *More Story Making!* with children for the first time, make one pattern book together as a group.

6. Have each child make a pattern book. (See pages 59–62 for procedures on creating pattern books.)

7. Encourage children to read their pattern books to each other.

8. Conduct one or more additional activities with students.

9. Direct children to take their pattern books home to read to family members or caregivers.

10. Complete the chosen form(s) for monitoring progress (from Appendix B) and the form for tracking use of the pattern books (Appendix C).

Monitoring Progress
Generic Form

Child Name: _____ **Grade:** _____

Goals: _____

_____

_____

_____

Pattern Book/Activities: _____

_____

Directions: List individual objectives in the left-hand column to meet the goals you list above. In the Comment columns, fill in the date and indicate the child's performance by checking the appropriate response. Make any additional comments.

Objectives	Comment	Comment	Comment
	Date: _____ ___ Mastered ___ Inconsistent ___ Emerging Comments:	Date: _____ ___ Mastered ___ Inconsistent ___ Emerging Comments:	Date: _____ ___ Mastered ___ Inconsistent ___ Emerging Comments:
	Date: _____ ___ Mastered ___ Inconsistent ___ Emerging Comments:	Date: _____ ___ Mastered ___ Inconsistent ___ Emerging Comments:	Date: _____ ___ Mastered ___ Inconsistent ___ Emerging Comments:
	Date: _____ ___ Mastered ___ Inconsistent ___ Emerging Comments:	Date: _____ ___ Mastered ___ Inconsistent ___ Emerging Comments:	Date: _____ ___ Mastered ___ Inconsistent ___ Emerging Comments:
	Date: _____ ___ Mastered ___ Inconsistent ___ Emerging Comments:	Date: _____ ___ Mastered ___ Inconsistent ___ Emerging Comments:	Date: _____ ___ Mastered ___ Inconsistent ___ Emerging Comments:

Monitoring Progress
Communication Rubric

Child Name: _____ **Grade:** _____

Goals: _____

_____

_____

_____

Pattern Book/Activities: _____

_____

Directions: List individual objectives in the left-hand column to meet the goals you list above. Then indicate the child's performance by dating and checking the appropriate response. In the remaining columns, list specific targets as appropriate.

Goals	Emerging	Inconsistent	Mastered
Use of phonological processes and production of speech sounds	**Student uses targets infrequently:** ❑ in single-word practice ❑ when reading a pattern story ❑ in conversation	**Student uses targets when reminded:** ❑ in single-word practice ❑ when reading a pattern story ❑ in conversation	**Student uses targets consistently and independently:** ❑ in single-word practice ❑ when reading a pattern story ❑ in conversation
Use of specific syntax structures	**Student uses correct forms infrequently:** ❑ in single-word practice ❑ when reading a pattern story ❑ in conversation	**Student uses correct forms when reminded:** ❑ in single-word practice ❑ when reading a pattern story ❑ in conversation	**Student uses correct forms consistently and independently:** ❑ in single-word practice ❑ when reading a pattern story ❑ in conversation
Use of specific concepts and vocabulary	**Student uses target words infrequently:** ❑ with a picture prompt ❑ with a story and picture prompt ❑ in conversation	**Student uses target words when reminded:** ❑ with a picture prompt ❑ with a story and picture prompt ❑ in conversation	**Student uses target words consistently and independently:** ❑ with a picture prompt ❑ with a story and picture prompt ❑ in conversation
Use of specific thinking skills	**Student demonstrates use of targeted thinking skills infrequently:** ❑ when talking about pictures ❑ when telling a story ❑ in conversation	**Student demonstrates use of targeted thinking skills when reminded:** ❑ when talking about pictures ❑ when telling a story ❑ in conversation	**Student demonstrates use of targeted thinking skills consistently and independently:** ❑ when talking about pictures ❑ when telling a story ❑ in conversation

Lesson Tracker

Pattern Books	Amanda, Amanda, What Did You Taste?	Animals Should Definitely Not	Blue Spaghetti and Meatballs	The Boat	Bubbles!	A Busy Farm	But Not Like Mine	Carly Bear, What Will You Wear?	Come and Play, Animal Friend!	Come and Play, Creature!	Come and Play, Friend!	A Dark, Dark Cave	Each Pickle Pumpkin Pie	Five Little Monkeys	For Sale	From Here to There	Hannah, Hannah, What Do You Hear?	Hi, Pizza Boy! (Animals)	Hi, Pizza Boy! (Seasonal Characters)	A Hot, Hot Desert	I Am Me! (Dogs)	I Am Me! (People)	I Am Me! (Transportation)	I Like You, Animals
Date of Use:																								
Group/Child:																								
Group/Child:																								
Group/Child:																								
Group/Child:																								
Group/Child:																								

Lesson Tracker—*Continued*

Pattern Books	*I Like You, Colors*	*Itchy, Itchy Mosquito Bites!*	*I Think I Can, I Think I Can! (Chores)*	*I Think I Can, I Think I Can! (Sports)*	*It's Not Safe!*	*I've Been Working at My School*	*I've Been Working on My House*	*Jolly Joshua*	*Kid's Day*	*My Pet Cat*	*My Pet Dog*	*One Bright Fall Morning*	*A-Riding We Will Go*	*A-Shopping We Will Go*	*Showy Shelly*	*The Sled*	*Stanley Gets Ready for School!*	*Time for Spring!*	*To the Zoo We'll Go*	*The Very Hungry Bear*	*What Moves in the Forest at Night?*	*Who Walks in the Zoo at Night?*	*Zicka Zicka Zoom Zoom!*
Date of Use:																							
Group/Child:																							
Group/Child:																							
Group/Child:																							
Group/Child:																							
Group/Child:																							

Parent Letter

Date: _____

Dear Parent,

_____ is bringing home a book that he or she made in school. The purpose of this book is to continue the learning process at home. Have your child read the story to you. If your child is not yet able to read, he or she can tell you about the story without saying the actual words on the page. This is acceptable and should not be corrected.

Your child is focusing on the following goals:

_____

_____

_____

_____

Listen to your child as he or she shares the book. If you notice your child mispronouncing a word or using a word incorrectly, say it correctly so that your child can hear the correct use. This technique is known as ***modeling.*** Modeling helps your child develop appropriate communication skills.

If you have any questions or concerns, please call me at _____. If there is a *Parent Feedback* form attached to this letter, please take time to reflect on your child's goals. This will help me gather accurate information about his or her communication skills at home. Thank you for your cooperation.

Sincerely,

_____

Parent Feedback

Date: _____

Dear Parent,

_____ is bringing home a book that he or she made in school. Please have your child read or tell the story to you. After your child is done, respond to the statements below to help me know more about his or her communication skills at home.

Check the responses that best describe the way your child read or told you about his or her book:

1. My child told me the story
   _____ with my help   _____ without my help
   Comments:

   _____

2. My child answered questions about the pictures in the book (for example, "What is that?", "What are they doing?", "Why would that happen?").

   _____ Yes   _____ No
   Comments:

   _____

3. My child pronounced words and sentences correctly.
   _____ Yes   _____ No (please explain)

   _____

4. Another book my child and I read this week was:

   _____

Thank you for completing this feedback form and returning it to me.

Sincerely,

_____

| **Please return by:** _____ |

Encouraging Literacy Skills at Home

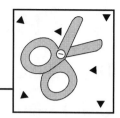

Date: _____

Dear Parent,

Reading and writing skills are also referred to as ***literacy skills.*** There are many activities and situations throughout the day that can encourage literacy development. The following are simple ways to encourage your child's literacy development and keep your child interested in reading and writing.

1. Read to your child on a regular basis. You may want to have a specific reading time set, but it should not be forced. If possible, the reading time should be one on one.

2. Designate a special area where you can go to read with your child. This place should have few distractions. Position your child so that he or she can see the book while you read.

3. Talk about the book you are reading. Take the time to answer questions as your child asks them. Relate the book to experiences you or your child have had.

4. Vary the pace of your reading and the volume of your voice when you read out loud. Remember to read slowly enough so that your child can build a picture of the action in his or her mind.

5. Point to the words as you read them so that your child can follow along. This will help him or her realize that a word is represented by a group of letters and that a space marks the beginning and end of a word.

(Over)

6. Read a variety of books with varying topics and lengths.

7. Reread books. Children tend to have favorite books that they want you to read again and again. This repetition is good for helping build skills such as memory, listening, and sequencing story parts and for building word knowledge. Each time children hear the story, they understand more about it. This helps them retell the story on their own.

8. Let your child tell stories to you. If needed, help him or her use and read new words.

9. Give your child lots of positive encouragement, rather than pointing out his or her communication errors. Then your child will enjoy the experience and want to read more. If your child mispronounces a word or uses a word incorrectly, model the correct form, but let your child continue the story.

10. Have writing supplies—paper and pencils—available for your child to use. He or she may want to draw pictures or write about things from the book you just read. (Note that writing can mean making marks on paper or writing simple words and sentences.)

11. Be enthusiastic about books yourself. One way to do this is to have your child see you reading books, newspapers, and magazines just for fun—not just because you have to.

12. Enjoy the time you and your child spend together, and have fun!

Sincerely,

Picture Index

Continued on next page

Picture Index—*Continued*

Continued on next page

373 © 2000 Thinking Publications

Picture Index—*Continued*

Continued on next page

    374

Picture Index—*Continued*

Continued on next page

Picture Index—*Continued*

Continued on next page

Picture Index—*Continued*

Continued on next page

377 © 2000 Thinking Publications

Picture Index—*Continued*

Miscellaneous Pictures

Using Interactive Language Charts

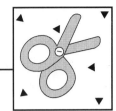

Creating an Interactive Language Chart

1. Write each sentence on a long strip of paper. (Leave a blank line for the word(s) that will change in each sentence.) Arrange the sentence strips in the correct order.

2. Glue the sentence strips onto a large piece of poster board. Pair words with pictures when possible (to facilitate word-recognition) by gluing pictures above their corresponding words. Enhance the chart with colorful drawings and/or designs, if desired. Laminate the poster board.

3. Create response cards by writing possible selections to complete the pattern phrases on small strips of poster board. Include a visual of each response by gluing a picture or drawing a corresponding illustration on each strip. (Consider color-coding rhyming words using colored paper.) Laminate the response cards.

4. Add Velcro to the back of each response card and above each blank line on the chart.

5. Attach a manila envelope to the back of the chart to store the response cards.

Conducting an Interactive Language Chart Activity

1. Display the chart and point to each word while reading the sentences to children. Encourage them to read along whenever possible.

2. Have children choose a response card and place it on the chart.

3. Read the sentences again, encouraging children to read along.

4. Continue to switch the response cards and read the sentences until all responses have been used.

© 2000 Thinking Publications

REFERENCES

Allington, R.L., and Cunningham, P.M. (1995). *Schools that work: Where all children read and write.* New York: Addison-Wesley.

Bankson, N., and Bernthal, J. (1990). *Bankson and Bernthal test of phonology.* Chicago: Riverside.

Bradshaw, M., Hoffman, P., and Norris, J. (1998). Efficacy of expansions and cloze procedures in the development of interpretations by preschool children exhibiting delayed language development. *Language, Speech, and Hearing Services in Schools, 29,* 85–95.

Catts, H. (1993). The relationship between speech-language impairments and reading disabilities. *Journal of Speech and Hearing Research, 36,* 948–958.

Creaghead, N. (1992). *Classroom language intervention: Developing schema for school success.* Buffalo, NY: Educom.

Fountas, I.C., and Pinnell, G.S. (1996). *Guided reading: Good first teaching for all children.* Portsmouth, NH: Heinemann.

Friel-Patti, S. (1998). Implications of auditory procession on emergent literacy. *Language Learning and Education, 5,* 25–26.

Gilbertson, M., and Bramlett, R. (1998). Phonological awareness screening to identify at-risk readers: Implications for practitioners. *Language, Speech, and Hearing Services in Schools, 29,* 109–116.

Gilbertson, M., and Thompson, E. (1997). Phonological awareness group education: PAGE. *The Clinical Connection, 10*(2), 14–16.

Gillon, G. (2000). The efficacy of phonological awareness intervention for children with spoken language impairment. *Language, Speech, and Hearing Services in Schools, 31,* 126–141.

Goldsworthy, C. (1996). *Developmental reading disabilities: A language based treatment approach.* San Diego, CA: Singular.

Goldsworthy, C. (1998). *Sourcebook of phonological awareness activities: Children's classic literature.* San Diego, CA: Singular.

Goodman, K. (1986). *What's whole in whole language?* Richmond Hill, Ontario: Scholastic-TAB Publications.

Goswami, U., and Bryant, P.E. (1990). *Phonological skills and learning to read.* Hillsdale, NJ: Erlbaum.

Hall, S., and Moats, L. (1999). *Straight talk about reading.* Chicago: Contemporary Books.

Haynes, W., and Shulman, B. (1994). *Communication development: Foundations, processes, and clinical applications.* Englewood Cliffs, NJ: Prentice Hall.

Hoggan, K., and Strong, C. (1994). The magic of "Once upon a time": Narrative teaching strategies. *Language, Speech, and Hearing Services in Schools, 25,* 76–89.

Johnson, T., and Louis, D. (1990). *Bringing it all together: A program for literacy.* Portsmouth, NH: Heinemann.

Kamhi, A., and Catts, H. (1991). Language and reading: Convergence, divergences, and development. In A. Kamhi and H. Catts (Eds.), *Reading disability: A developmental language perspective* (pp. 1–35, 369–379). Needham Heights, MA: Allyn and Bacon.

Koppenhaver, D.A., Coleman, P.P., Kalman, S.L., and Yoder, D.E. (1991). The implications of emergent literacy research for children with developmental disabilities. *American Journal of Speech-Language Pathology, 1*(1), 38–44.

Larson, V. Lord, and McKinley, N. (1995). *Language disorders in older students: Preadolescents and adolescence.* Eau Claire, WI: Thinking Publications.

Liberman, I.Y., Shankweiler, D., Fischer, F.W., and Carter, B. (1974). Reading and the awareness of linguistic segments. *Journal of Experimental Child Psychology, 18,* 201–212.

Lombardino, L., Riccio, C., Hynd, G., and Pinheiro, S. (1997). Linguistic deficits in children with reading disabilities. *American Journal of Speech-Language Pathology, 6*(3), 71–78.

Luedeker, L. (1996). Ensuring success for the beginning reader. In J. Baltas and S. Shafer (Eds.), *Scholastic guide to balanced reading (K–2): Making it work for you* (pp. 43–48). New York: Scholastic.

Martinez, M., and Roser, N. (1985). Read it again: The value of repeated readings during storytime. *The Reading Teacher, 38,* 782–786.

Marvin, C. (1994). Home literacy experience of preschool children with single and multiple disabilities. *Topics in Early Childhood Special Education, 14*(4), 436–454.

Marvin, C., and Mirenda, P. (1992). *Early literacy opportunities for preschool children with disabilities.* Unpublished manuscript, University of Nebraska, Lincoln.

Marvin, C., and Privratsky, A. (1999). After-school talk: The effects of materials sent home from preschool. *American Journal of Speech-Language Pathology, 8*(3), 231–240.

Marvin, C., and Wright, D. (1997). Literacy socialization in the homes of preschool children. *Language, Speech, and Hearing Services in Schools, 28,* 154–163.

McFadden, T. (1998). Sounds and stories: Teaching phonemic awareness in interactions around text. *American Journal of Speech-Language Pathology, 7*(2), 5–13.

Montgomery, J. (1993, October). *Whole language + speech pathologists + classroom teachers = collaboration!* Paper presented at the Whole Language Workshop, Milwaukee, WI.

Morrow, L.M., and O'Connor, E.M. (1995). Literacy partnerships for change with "at-risk" kindergartners. In R.L. Allington and S.A. Walmsley (Eds.), *No quick fix: Rethinking literacy programs in America's elementary schools* (pp. 97–115). New York: Teachers College Press.

Nelson, N. (1994). Curriculum-based language assessment and intervention across the grades. In G. Wallach and K. Butler (Eds.), *Language learning disabilities in school-age children and adolescents: Some principles and applications* (pp. 104–131). New York: Macmillan.

Norris, J., and Damico, J. (1990). Whole language in theory and practice: Implications for language intervention. *Language, Speech, and Hearing Services in Schools, 21,* 212–220.

Norris, J., and Hoffman, P. (1993). *Whole language intervention for school-age children.* San Diego, CA: Singular.

Owens, R., and Robinson, L. (1997). Once upon a time: Use of children's literature in the preschool classroom. *Topics in Language Disorders, 17*(2), 19–48.

Peura, R., and DeBoer, C. (1995). *Story making: Using predictable literature to develop communication.* Eau Claire, WI: Thinking Publications.

Rivers, K., Lombardino, L., and Thompson, C. (1996). Effects of phonological decoding training on children's word recognition of CVC, CV, and VC structures. *American Journal of Speech-Language Pathology, 5*(1), 67–78.

Routman, R. (1991). *Invitations: Changing as teachers and learners K–12.* Portsmouth, NH: Heinemann.

Schraeder, T., Quinn, M., Stockman, I.J., and Miller, J. (1999). Authentic assessment as an approach to preschool speech-language screening. *American Journal of Speech-Language Pathology, 8*(3), 195–200.

Secord, W.A. (1999, September). *Team-based assessment and intervention.* Paper presented to the Hamilton County Board of Mental Retardation, Clermont County Educational Service Center, and Hamilton County Educational Service Center, Cincinnati, OH.

Simon, C.S. (1991). Communication skills and classroom success: Some considerations for assessment and therapy methodologies. In C.S. Simon (Ed.), *Communication skills and classroom success* (pp. 1–77). Eau Claire, WI: Thinking Publications.

Snow, C., Scarborough, H., and Burns, M. (1999). What speech-language pathologists need to know about early reading. *Topics in Language Disorders, 20*(1), 48–58.

Stackhouse, J. (1997). Phonological awareness: Connecting speech and literacy problems. In B.W. Hodson and M.L. Edwards (Eds.), *Perspectives in applied phonology* (pp. 157–196). Gaithersburg, MD: Aspen.

Stainback, S., and Stainback, W. (1992). *Curriculum considerations and inclusive classrooms: Facilitating learning for all students.* Baltimore: Brookes.

Stanovich, K., Cunningham, A., and Freeman, D. (1984). Intelligence, cognitive skills, and early reading progress. *Reading Research Quarterly, 19,* 279–303.

Sulzby, E. (1989). Forms of writing and rereading from writing. In J. Mason (Ed.), *Reading and writing connections* (pp. 51–63). Needham Heights, MA: Allyn and Bacon.

Swank, L., and Catts, H. (1994). Phonological awareness and written word decoding. *Language, Speech, and Hearing Services in Schools, 25,* 9–14.

van Kleeck, A. (1990). Emergent literacy: Learning about print before learning to read. *Topics in Language Disorders, 10*(2), 25–45.

van Kleeck, A. (1994). Metalinguistic development. In G. Wallach and K. Butler (Eds.), *Language and learning disabilities in school-age children and adolescents: Some principles and applications* (pp. 53–103). New York: Merrill.

van Kleeck, A. (1995). Emphasizing form and meaning separately in prereading and early reading instruction. *Topics in Language Disorders, 16*(1), 27–49.

van Kleeck, A., Gillam, R., and McFadden, T. (1998). A study of classroom-based phonological awareness training for preschoolers with speech and/or language disorders. *American Journal of Speech-Language Pathology, 7*(3), 65–76.

Wallach, G., and Butler, K. (Eds.). (1994). *Language and learning disorders in school-age children and adolescents: Some principles and applications.* New York: Merrill.

Wallach, G., and Miller, L. (1988). *Language intervention and academic success.* Newton, MA: Butterworth Heinemann.

Watson, L., Layton, T., Pierce, P., and Abraham, L. (1994). Enhancing emerging literacy in a language preschool. *Language, Speech, and Hearing Services in Schools, 25,* 136–145.

Westby, C. (1991). Learning to talk-talking to learn: Oral-literate language differences. In C.S. Simon (Ed.), *Communication skills and classroom success* (pp. 334–357). Eau Claire, WI: Thinking Publications.

Westby, C. (1998). Language in critical literacy: Issues in LLD, ADHD, and dyslexia. *Language Learning and Education, 5,* 22–24.

Wetherby, A. (1992). *Communication and language intervention for preschool children.* Buffalo, NY: Educom.

Yopp, H.K. (1992). Developing phonemic awareness in young children. *The Reading Teacher, 45*(9), 696–703.

Spooky
PUZZLES

Burton Marks
Illustrated by Amelia Rosato

HOW TO USE YOUR PUZZLE DECODER

To unscramble the wacky words and find the hidden ghosts, goblins, and spooks in the book you must use the magic mirror on your Puzzle Decoder. Place the edge of your mirror along a dotted line. The reflection in the mirror will reveal the clue.

If you see a double set of dotted lines that run up and down, place the edge of your magic mirror along either line.

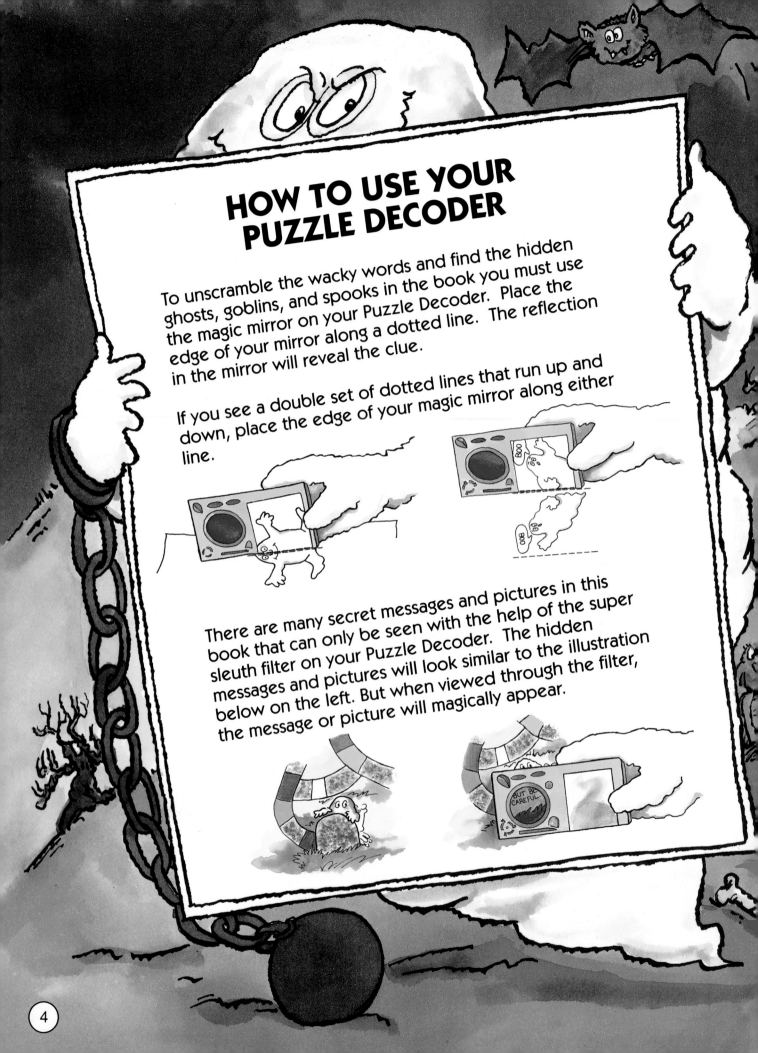

There are many secret messages and pictures in this book that can only be seen with the help of the super sleuth filter on your Puzzle Decoder. The hidden messages and pictures will look similar to the illustration below on the left. But when viewed through the filter, the message or picture will magically appear.

COME TO HAUNTED HILL...

...if you dare. Four treasures are hidden there — each one guarded by a ghost. The treasures are a gold chest, a king's crown, a diamond necklace, and a ruby ring. Your job is to find the treasures and the four ghosts who guard them. You get five points for each treasure you find and five points for each ghost. If you collect a total of 40 points, you are a winner. Start your quest on the next page. Be sure to take your Puzzle Decoder with you. You'll need it to work out all the ghostly clues.

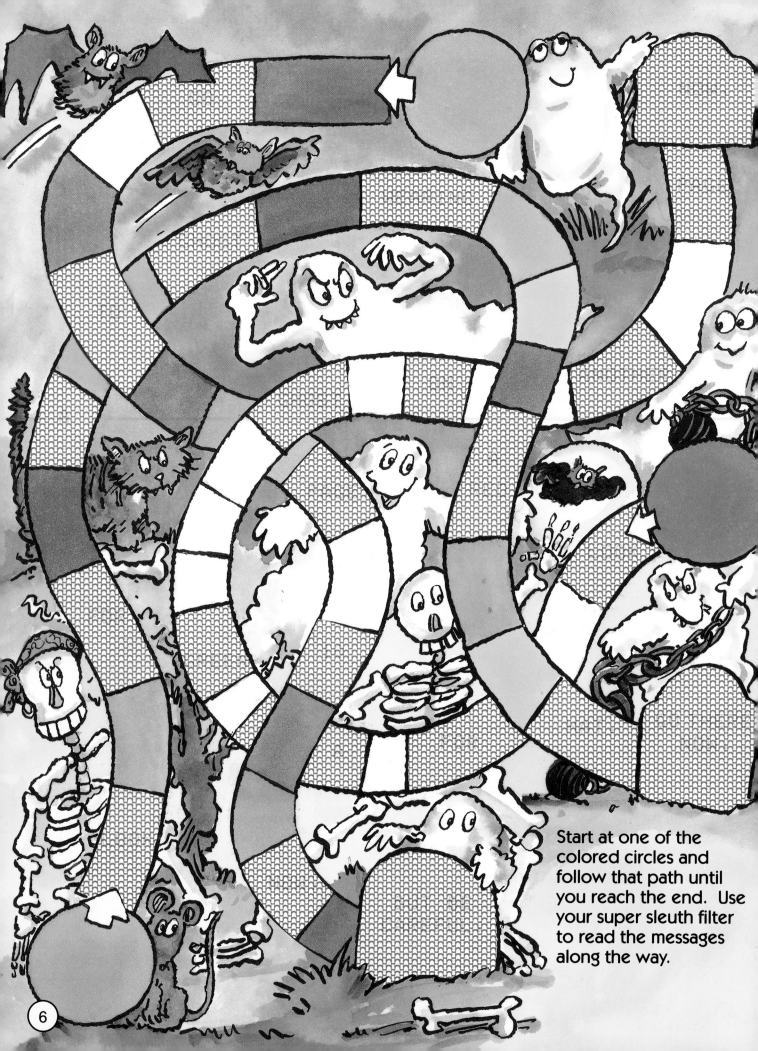

Start at one of the
colored circles and
follow that path until
you reach the end. Use
your super sleuth filter
to read the messages
along the way.

The ruby ring is somewhere in this room. Using your super sleuth filter, try to find four letters that are hidden in the pictures on the walls. Then use your magic mirror to see what the ghost has to say.

Use the 4 letters to spell the name of a color. Then look for an object below that is that color. The ring is now close to that color. Use your super sleuth filter to find it.

If you find the ruby ring, collect 5 points. Then go to page 6 and start on the orange circle.

SPOOKY SEARCH

Meet two very spooky ghosts. You can create new ghosts from them by holding your magic mirror along the dotted lines. First look at one side of the mirror, then the other.

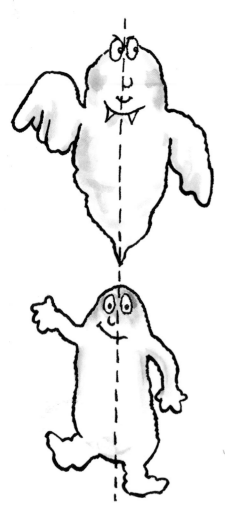

One of the new ghosts you will see appears somewhere in this room. It is one of the ghosts you are looking for. If you find it, collect 5 points.

The diamond necklace is also somewhere in this room.
To find it, use your super sleuth filter to search for clues.
If you find the necklace, collect 5 points. Then go to
page 6 and start on the blue circle.

RIDDLE ROMP

Each of these spooks is tellling a riddle. Use your magic mirror to read it. Then follow the string that the spook is holding. At the end of the string is the answer to the riddle. Your super sleuth filter will reveal what it is.

The answer to one of the riddles will lead you to the king's crown.

WHAT JEWELS DO SPOOKS WEAR?

WHY WAS THE GHOST ARRESTED?

WHERE DO GHOSTS LIVE?

11

SPOOKS' GOLD

The gold chest is hidden somewhere here. You can find it by following a set of clues. To find your first clue, look for a spook with orange hair. That spook is flying an invisible kite. Your first clue is written on the kite.

Use your super sleuth filter to find the kite and each of the other clues you come to.

If you find the gold chest, collect 5 points. Then read this message in your magic mirror.

RUBY RING.
ON THE WAY TO FINDING THE
GO NOW TO PAGE 21. YOU ARE

13

SECRET  PASSAGE

These mysterious underground passages hold many secrets. If you dare to enter, you will learn where the gold chest is hidden.

Place your mirror on the dotted line to read these instructions.

- -

TO READ THE MESSAGE IN IT,
USE YOUR SUPER STEALTH FILTER
WHEN YOU COME TO A CIRCLE.
START AT THE ARROW BELOW.

14

GHOST PARTY

One of the ghosts you are looking for is shown here. You can tell which one it is because he is also attending the party below. The only problem you may have is that, like so many ghosts at the party, he is invisible.

Here's how to find the ghost. Place your magic mirror along the dotted line at the left. Then slowly move the mirror to the right until the ghost appears.

If you find the ghost, collect 5 points. Then go to page 6 and start on the green circle.

CASTLE WALK

Start at the arrow and take a walk through the castle. Use your super sleuth filter to read what the ghosts have to say along the way. If you dare to finish the walk, you will learn the whereabouts of the king's crown.

If you find the king's crown, collect 5 points.
Then read this message in your magic mirror.

GO NOW TO PAGE 19. A GHOST
YOU SEEK IS LURKING THERE.

17

Place your magic mirror along the dotted line at the right and a ghost's name will appear. A ghost with the same name is hiding below. It is one of the ghosts you are looking for. See if you can find it with your super sleuth filter.

BOOHOO

If you find the correct ghost, collect 5 points. Then look for a number on that ghost's hat. You should go to that page next. Another ghost you seek is hiding there.

18

MIRROR SPOOK

Hold your magic mirror along each dotted line. The reflection of one of these ghosts appears below. It is one of the ghosts you are looking for. See how quickly you can find it.

If you find the ghost, collect 5 points. Then go to page 15. Another ghost you seek is there.

VANISHING ACT

Only ONE of the eight spooks in the house below will disappear before your eyes when viewed through the super sleuth filter. That spook appears on another page. He will help you find the ruby ring.

ANSWER PAGE

Page 6 The ghost wearing the red hat is on page 18. The green ghost is on page 20.

Page 7 The hidden letters are E, L, U, and B. When rearranged, they spell the word BLUE. The ruby ring is hidden in the blue chest on the table.

Pages 8 & 9 This is the ghost you are looking for:

The diamond necklace can be found behind the skull on the right side of the fireplace.

Answer: Pages 8&9.

Pages 10 & 11 The riddle that you are seeking is: *Where is the best place to hide a king's crown?* The answer is: *On page 16.*

Pages 12 & 13 The gold chest is hidden in front of the fence to the right of the castle.

Page 15 This is the ghost you are looking for:

If you move the magic mirror to the right about 5 inches, that ghost will appear.

Answer: Page 15.

Pages 16 & 17 This is the message of the ghosts: TO FIND THE CROWN LOOK BEHIND THE BLUE DOOR.

Page 18 The ghost's name is BOOHOO. The ghost with that name is standing on the steps. The number on his hat is 8.

Page 19 The ghost you are seeking is wearing a necktie and a hat. He is carrying a sign that says HOWDY.

Page 20 The hidden numbers add up to 14.

Page 21 The ghost that disappears can also be found on page 7.